# BOOGIE
# LIGHTNING

Also by Michael Lydon:  *Rock Folk*
*Greenwood* (editor)

by MICHAEL LYDON

hotographs by Ellen Mandel

he Dial Press New York 1974

The photographs are by Ellen Mandel except that of Ralph Bass on page 80, which is by American Passport Studio, and the photographs of The Action on page 122, which are from a 1965 contact sheet by Leslie Bryce.

Library of Congress Cataloging in Publication Data
Lydon, Michael.
Boogie Lightning.
1. Jazz musicians. 2. Phonograph. I. Title.
ML394.L95  785.4′2′0922 [B]  73–18111
ISBN 0–8037–2061–0

Manufactured in the United States of America
First printing, 1974

for Ellen

> . . . *a pretty bird,*
> *Golden as a honey bee*

# CONTENTS

# BOOGIE LIGHTNING

The name electricity is applied to an invisible agent known only by the effects which it produces, and the many ways in which it manifests itself.

—Frank D. Graham,
*Audels' Engineers and Mechanics Guide #8.*

Sometimes I sit here in this chair and I wonder.

—Ray Charles

● The purpose of this book is to prove the reality of a historical event: the wedding of music and electricity, a ceremony enacted by black American musicians of the popular sort. The union, in the making since the turn of the century, was consummated at the century's mid-point, and in the two decades since has borne fruit with an astounding fertility.

The eighteenth century's experimental investigations into

INTRODUCTION

the properties of electrical energy led, in the nineteenth, to the first tentative applications of its awesome power. Electricity, it was discovered, traveled at great speed and in a wavelike fashion; although dispersed universally in every form and level of matter, its flow could be conducted on specific voyages along paths of man's own choosing. Upon this swift "current" patterns could be imposed. Any suitable valvelike device could, like the Indian's blanket over a column of smoke, interrupt the flow and introduce into it a patterned pulse comprised of surges of varying electrical strength. Despite the liquid metaphors used by the adventurers who first noted these mysterious phenomena, electrical currents, unlike water in a pipe, could maintain these patterns indefinitely and with an extraordinarily articulate fidelity to the impulse that created them. Moreover, when the current had reached its destination, the power of the electrical flow could move a similar valve to recreate the impulse which had set the pattern of the pulse at the trip's beginning. This second impulse, though an image of the first, had a degree of similarity to its original that seemed magically "real."

Electricity's marvelous ability to recreate actions in precise and "real" images far removed from the original action began to have communicative use with the telegraph. The telegraph's urgent rhythm of clicks and clickety-clicks was a kind of music; those clicks embodied, indeed were, discrete and understandable units of information which, though they had written counterparts, were directly apprehendable to the experienced ear. It was not long before the eager explorers of the late Victorian era went beyond this mechanical on-off system. Essentially the same process, they discovered, allowed the transmission and amplification of any sound. Nor was that all; the sound did not need to go directly from aural impulse to aural image but could be converted into and stored as stylus writing on "wax," a physical record of itself; then it could be released as sound at any time. Finally, and perhaps most marvelous, men found that these patterns need not even be conducted: they could be released into the universal dispersion of electricity and even from there, a whole world away, be recaptured and made to deliver their message.

Two decades into the twentieth century all of these inventions—the telephone, microphone and loudspeaker, phonograph, and wireless radio—had come into common use. That the twentieth would be the electric century had passed from prophecy into cliché. Change was everywhere, and despite those who viewed this "progress" as dangerous, blasphemous, or both, electricity was integrated into ordinary life with a celerity that many ascribed to the nature of the power which had apparently been so easily tamed. Men and women who could not have conceived of the telephone or phonograph as children soon forgot how they had done without them. The world-transforming electrical inventions seem to have become an integral part of the lives of their first users so swiftly as to have by-passed full consciousness. Had people understood the threshold they were crossing—had it been less dazzling or sold to them with less hoopla—perhaps they would have been slower crossing it. Once irrevocably across, however, people found it comforting to think that though all had changed, nothing had *really* changed.

This integration without complete awareness is well illustrated in music's reaction to electrification. Music, built on laws as elemental as anything we know, is profoundly conservative. So ancient is it that "new" music often seems but each era's reinterpretation and reflection on its timeless values. Music has its own history, as does science or law, a history of movements and geniuses, brilliant eras and stagnant ones, challenges encountered and problems solved. This history has a life of its own: music, closely related to mathematics in the abstract precision of its language, can transcend the limitations of time-bound culture. On the other hand, music is no less bound to day-to-day time than fashion. Music springs from the whole lives of those who make it and changes as they and their environments change. Bach's music, for instance, has not simply been "interpreted" differently over the centuries through which it has lived so gloriously, but all sorts of different people, some in nineteenth-century London, others in twentieth-century Los Angeles, have experienced it as they liked best.

Music's conservatism did not, however, stop twentieth-century musicians and music lovers from accepting the opportunities of electric technology, just as they bought toasters and refrigerators. From the first the phonograph, radio, and microphone-loudspeaker were so admirably suited to music that, as media, they became primarily associated with it. Couples found they could dance and kiss in the parlor to the Victrola as well as in the shadows of the bandstand, and lucky musicians took all the studio work they could get, particularly because it paid better than restaurant or theater jobs. Some even made electrical instruments, and "daring" composers began to work with the unknown tonalities of electronic sound (these experiments had minimal public acceptance, even in music circles, until the 1950s). Electricity's changes could be accepted as "social and economic progress"; that way their challenge to purely musical values could be blunted or ignored altogether. A violinist of the 1920s and 1930s, even though employed in a radio orchestra and moonlighting recording dates, believed that musically nothing "real" had changed since the days of his teacher, who had known nothing but live performance. Mozart was Mozart, our violinist's conservative instincts would have told him, in the concert hall or before the grey metal ears of the microphones. He was, after all, playing the same instrument and reading the same notation; could context be banished, he was doing the same thing.

Context could not be banished, nor even held at bay for long. The violinist was breaching musical laws as time-honored as the Aristotelian unities. Music, more than any other art, was the art of here and now. Its concept of time was not only that of tempo, but of immediate and immediately passing creation. Its space, though metaphysically universal, was in practice that within earshot. Though it had come far from the chants of storytellers and shamans, music's mode of action was still conversational—

an experience shared by those gathered to share it. Electricity's intervention changed all that. Assisted by loudspeakers, music could be more a speech than a conversation; on record it could be preserved forever instead of dying at birth; radio broadcast it past all known boundaries. Live music is powerfully visual as well as aural—the brass look the way they sound; a radio or phonograph looks the same transmitting Vivaldi or nothing.

Moreover, what was heard in Dubuque of the violinist's sawings in New York was not the sound of his violin but that sound's image. The sound of that image was made not by a violin but by the rapid pulsations of a paper cone responding to patterned surges of electrical power. This electrical "speaker" had sounds of its own—static, hisses, and clicks—and the listener, not the musician, controlled it. Utterly without discrimination, the new instrument relayed and recreated any sound with equal ease. As an image maker, it could substitute "false" image for "true"— what sounded like thunder was probably anything but. Indeed, this system could vary any characteristic of a sound between original and final image, and the heard sequence of sound might bear no resemblance to the sequence of original creation.

Electricity had not been tamed, only leashed. Its energy could transform music's essential nature. From its first challenge to music's traditional immediacy and intimacy, it offered possibilities which, if seized, could open a new musical era. How to seize them? Could these electric sound images be made to yield a music of their own? What music could retain freshness despite "canning"? Could that distant radio be not simply a receiver but a playable and sympathetic instrument on its own? How to make the quantum leap from the eternal past of "acoustic" music to the uncharted future of "electric" music? The tiger could be ridden, but could rider and steed become one?

When Benjamin Franklin sent up a kite and unlocked a thunderstorm with a key, the black-skinned people who lived in America were legally subhuman. Not here of their own will, they were innocent victims of the unstoppable growth of European empires, whose builders, trading with populated Africa and needing workers in barren America, did the logical with the efficiency of greed. The voyage from Africa's tribal home to the cold bosom of America's "peculiar institution" began with betrayal and enchained captivity for the march to the sea; there men newly become slaves were sold and shipped across the ocean as cargo. On arrival they were sold again, and perhaps again, coming to rest as the personal possessions of men whose eyes refused to see through skin to kinship. The trauma was as complete as any imaginable, and the terms of its insanity were upheld with every power the captor had at his command. That an identity could survive such agony is miraculous; yet as anyone knows who has even momentarily been able to share the black perspective, it's the white folks who seem crazy.

An identity—a point of view, a sense of humor—did survive, not in everyone, at times not in many, but in enough. Slavery in a foreign land was the low point; when down looked up, only one direction was possible. African became slave became American slave became freed American slave became American black man, each step hard and all victories dubious. Any identity is at best a quest for identity, and the black American's quest has been waylaid by the fiercest demons of internal and external reality. Recovery and assertion of self continued; what can only be called the collective consciousness of American black people grew from numbed passivity to a restive, self-challenging awareness. The memory of slavery was a goad, freedom an inspiration. Only struggle could expand a black man's space in which to express his pain and beauty. Hearts were broken, minds crushed, yet with each decade that space grew larger.

Music has ever been the most striking expression of black American identity. Black people sang at work, at play, and at prayer; what a black man sang, he was. As his sphere of action and sense of self grew, and his experience became more varied, so did his music grow and diversify. In 1800 there were few black "musicians." By 1900 there were minstrels with their banjos, revivalists with their tambourines, touring choirs of spiritual singers, washboard virtuosi in Birmingham, cornetists and piano players in Storyville, guitarists in Mississippi, tap-dancing shoeshine boys in the lobbies of Memphis hotels—black American music was, as historians would say, a nascent but vital institution.

Growth brought the music increasingly into contact with "white" music—an older and perhaps less flexible institution, but also expressive of a multifaceted identity. When white Americans heard black music their reactions ran the gamut yet were one: disbelief. How did they get those amazing sounds? Black music had an elan, a swing—"that crazy beat"—which was startlingly original and undeniably effective. Intrigued, white musicians tried to get the hang of it. Many stole, more copied; a few borrowed with respect, and fewer still made the sounds their own way. Played by whites, black music spread everywhere, becoming the most distinctive color in the racial and historical quilt of American music. Black musicians, who had a harder time finding jobs, and with their own musical past only half-remembered, took what they needed from the white heritage: the structure of the hymn and ballad, the English language, and, above all, the instruments. What the American Negro did with the saxophone, trumpet and even violin had theretofore been considered musically illegal; what they did with the voice, impossible. By the 1920s jazz was internationally recognized as a new music.

The black musician used the electric media as did other musicians, recording and broadcasting when he could. His music, only slightly older than the new inventions, took to them well: its spontaneous, improvised quality made even its image vital. Yet if musical values did not limit the black musician's freedom with these new instruments, social realities did. Electric guitars, the first popularly manufactured electric instruments, came to black musicians five, even ten years later than to whites simply because they were expensive and needed connection to a power source. The linked businesses of recording and radio broadcasting had become an electric music industry by the early 1940s; black Americans, though sporadically used as musicians and wooed as customers, had as little to say in this capitalist enterprise as in any other.

The Depression drove the black man from the country, World War II sucked him to the city; landless peasant became wage slave. The city changed the black man as it changes everyone, quickening activity and heightening contrasts. After the war, though isolated in the ghetto, Negroes, with the new capital *N*, were cash-carrying members of the national economy. As a marginal market, they attracted marginal businessmen, some of whom saw money in music. An independent—nearly underground—record business started in the ghetto. Its shoestring studios were uptown; in them black musicians who had been children before the war played with a nakedness discouraged elsewhere. The records they made, though aimed at a black audience, started selling to whites and, despite discouragement, crept onto radio; some black men even became disc jockeys.

And then, what? Suddenly and for millions, these records had an excitement, a mysterious something that even the hottest jazz sides had not contained. They sounded "loud" even when soft, became all-encompassing when truly loud. Was it the exaggerated beat, the frenetic vocals, the comically unintelligible lyrics, the built-in echoes and "distortions," the electric guitars? Or was it the sexuality, the invocations to release and dance, the undercurrent of menace? In and of themselves these records were fascinating musical experiences, induplicable and self-contained. They were not recordings of music; the song, the performance recorded, and the process of recording and record distribution all contributed to the music of the record.

Simultaneously, recording was undergoing innovations which amounted to a rebirth—magnetic tape, long-playing unbreakable discs, cheap 45s, and high fidelity. Musicians of all kinds began to record more often for markets which were growing larger by the month. Yet hi-fi jazz was still jazz, long-playing Brahms still Brahms, and the pop tunes on the Hit Parade still but the popular songs of the day. What was new musically were these rhythm records on independent labels, and by the early 1950s the response to them was a running page-one story. Straining to equal the intensity of the new records, radio broadcasters forewent the conversational approach and began to treat the country's radios as their personal loudspeakers. The power of the music did not diminish off record and radio; in amplified live performance it created a new theater. A new audience became apparent; its relationship with its artistic alter egos was marked by a passion which, if sometimes fickle, was often felt as life-changing. The music, its media, and its listeners —by 1956 they were known to be an entity, though with disputable characteristics. What the entity was was a mystery; nothing like it had ever been seen before. It was named rock 'n' roll music.

Music had become electric. With the same felicitious abandon which had marked his creation of a new musical world for the harmonica and washtub, the black American began to play electricity. What Sidney Bechet and Louis Armstrong had done to the clarinet and trumpet, an epic generation of bluesmen did to the electric guitar. Black people at mid-century were beginning to speak in public as they spoke in private; this meant, musically, that they were able not only to play in the privacy of the studio, but to use the studio as a public, even global, stage. The "grooves" and "airwaves" were no longer heavy trains bearing acoustic music as freight, but the mercurial agents of a new form of musical communication.

Such a moment did not go unnoticed in the music world. Like many breakthroughs long in coming, it was followed by an onrush. Many talented and energetic musicians came to the fore; by no means all were black. What was a trickle became a river. There was resistance. It was not only a few critics and academicians who ignored or excoriated rock 'n' roll, but a complex and pervasive mentality which rock 'n' roll unsettled. This mentality, acting as a cultural superego, lumped aesthetic, social, and racial judgments into a frontal negative to the music as anything but the folly of youth or the growls of the underdog. Even the businessmen who were not hesitant in taking their profits from it considered it backdoor trade until those profits built new and grander front doors for their businesses. Today, despite—or is it now because of?—rock 'n' roll's musical successes, snobberies still linger. Yet rock 'n' roll has, in opening music to a new spectrum of possible sounds, helped steer musical values back to their primeval source in sensual-mystical delight. It is still young.

I wish to prove the above true. I will be striking keys, much, I hope, as a harpist plucks her strings. My proof, successful or not, is but a fiction. May it do well. Proofs are the better for their elegance, I am told, but I bar no holds. Boogie!

● "The world," said John Lee Hooker, "is a natural-born jungle." A stew bubbled on the yellow stove. Bright California winter sunshine beamed through net curtains. Hooker stood in his kitchen. His arms, long for his small, almost childlike body, hung relaxed at his sides, his hands lined and pulpy soft. He had on a bright red shirt, nondescript brown pants, and suede rubber-soled shoes. No belt. His brown eyes were quiet, his black

JOHN LEE HOOKER

face clear. On his head was a skinny-brim hat of horsehide. He turned to the stove, lifted the lid of the stew, smelled hard, and grinned. As he straightened up, his thought came back to him. A slow sadness moved over his face. "People don't know which way to go. They are confused. Lost in this world. That is what I see. Race against race, religion against religion, people fighting. It is hard to explain."

In the living room, resting on an aquamarine expanse of wall-to-wall, was a Florentine-style phonograph console rigged up with flashing red and blue light panels. One of his recent albums was on at medium volume. A nice lick caught his ear. "That, that was Steve Miller." The phone rang.

"Hello. Yes, this is John Lee." He stood still, concentrated on his unseen caller. "Oh yeah, baby, you back in town?" He asked for the friend's number and indicated that I was to write it down. "Six-two-seven, five-four-oh-nine? Okay, baby, come over sometime I'm home."

He sat down at the table. "Now where was we at? Yeah. My music is the blues. It tells my story, my problems. People can listen, maybe it'll help them solve their problems. We could be one happy family in this world. We're in it together, enough room for everybody." He looked straight at me. "We're not here to stay, you know, we is just passing through."

In 1948, as John Lee Hooker remembers, a man named El-mer Barbara lived at 609 Lafayette Street in Detroit, Michigan. Barbara owned a small record store and in the back had a primitive record-cutting lathe, on which he could make passable dubs. Like most such, the store was a musicians' hang-out, and Barbara, a watchful sentry at the recording industry's remotest border, fancied himself a talent scout. That a Bing Crosby would stroll in wasn't likely, but a future Inkspot or Louis Jordan might. Who knew what made for success in the record biz? To Barbara and many others, some facts were obvious.

Negroes bought records when they could afford to, and in

1948 more could than ever before. Equally important from a businessman's point of view, they were reachable as a market. Selling to black Americans before the war had been by mail order or by small-order salesmanship on backwoods routes out of Willy Loman's nightmares. Negroes were nickel-and-dime, cross-the-tracks trade, by-passed by the economy's mainstream; only the astute had made fortunes from them. After the war, however, millions of Negroes were living in the big cities of the North, Midwest, and West. All the pressures that impel migration had been at work, and once again a rural people oppressed by poverty and a traditional caste system moved to the promise of cash and opportunity in the city. Cousins followed stepbrothers to Chicago; nephews were sent to live with aunts in Minneapolis; sailors in San Francisco never got back to Lithonia and Waycross, Georgia; families packed up Fords; and young men rode freight trains away from pregnant girlfriends. The city fulfilled few dreams, but even the disillusioned seldom went back.

These were Negroes a business could get to, concentrated in numbers large enough to make a bulk operation profitable. They didn't have much money, but they spent what they did have on fast-turnover consumer items. Urban blacks constituted a growing specialty market, and little guys like Barbara saw its prospects before the big companies did. Barbara had more new customers in his store than he had new records to sell them. The major record companies had let their race catalogues atrophy in the war years; they still recorded jazz irregularly and pushed only that black music which had an equal if not predominant white appeal. The tiny labels which had grown up when vinyl was scarce in the early 1940s delivered good discs but not steadily—only hits kept these companies going, and when they did have hits, they often couldn't get enough records pressed and to the stores.

It made sense for Barbara to help supply himself by getting records made that he could sell. There was available talent. In the migration had come musicians—not many jazzmen or band-trained players, who could read charted arrangements and get jobs in Detroit's established music market, but blues singers, pickers, blowers, and thumpers. Though a few of these had eked out livings playing professionally in the South, most had played whenever and for whatever they could. Their music, sometimes raw, sometimes elegant, was fiercely individual and made little or no reference to the musics then deemed popular. In the South the bluesmen had chopped cotton by day and played at barbecues and fish fries at night; they swept offices and washed cars in the North, playing the bars around midnight. They had arrived with their audience—get them on wax and a record business was ready-made.

"I came to Detroit in 1942, when I was about twenty," said John Lee. "Originally I'm from Clarksdale, Mississippi, the Delta. Now I haven't been back there for a *long* time. I started playing the guitar when I was thirteen years old. I learned from my stepfather, Willy Moore. The style I play now, he played then. Too bad he never made anything out of it." Moore was an accomplished blues guitarist, and the young John Lee heard not only him, but Blind Lemon Jefferson, Charlie Patton, and others who came to play at Moore's house. When he left the Delta for Memphis at fourteen, he believed he was good. Memphis didn't care, so he moved on to Cincinnati. He left there for Detroit and war work in the booming motor factories. He had never stopped playing, and after the war he started getting jobs in the clubs along Detroit's Hastings Street. At times he had a small group with him; mostly he worked alone.

"I had heard that this Elmer Barbara was cutting local guys who played guitar and harmonica, stuff like that. I walked in one day. He worked with me night and day for months, cutting dubs and trying different experiments. But he didn't have the setup to make real records, so when we had something that was good I took it to Bernard Besman. I didn't know Besman, but he was a record distributor who also had a label, the Sensation label. He liked the dub, and I started working with him."

Bernard Besman, then about thirty, was a small frog in the

next-bigger pond. A pianist who loved the rippling swing of Earl "Fatha" Hines but as Dean Dennis played a commercially passable imitation of Carmen Cavallero, he had, even before the war, been more drawn to the business of music than to a performing career. In the army Besman booked bands for the Special Services, and after discharge he teamed up with an accountant friend to distribute records in Michigan for the Los Angeles-based Pan American label. In 1972, in North Hollywood himself and in the toy business—his company had the Bozo the Clown merchandising franchise—he remembered his Detroit days with a phlegmatic pleasure.

"Playing music and selling records, I found out, are two different things," he said, sitting on a back-office couch. "In 1946 we got a little store on Linwood Avenue, did well from the start. Rafael Mendez, a trumpet player, had a hit on Pan American, so did Eddie Cantor. But one label wasn't enough to keep us going, so we got the Exclusive label: Joe Liggams of 'The Honeydripper' was with Exclusive; Johnny Moore; and that blues singer Charles Brown, he was on it too. Then we got Modern and Aladdin. With them we had the three big race labels. The white stores wouldn't take their stuff; I'd say it went to an 85 to 90 percent black audience. It sold because before us those records weren't available in Detroit except by special order, and there were about half a million Negroes in the city then. We were doing twenty-two thousand dollars a month at the end of the first year."

Distribution got the product to the store; the problem was to get the customer in to buy it. Radio was the obvious answer— a record played is its own advertisement—so obvious that the big record companies tried to make sure only their products got aired. What freedom of choice they did not discourage, the stalwarts of the musicians' union, anxious to keep their broadcast-orchestra jobs, did—they were trying to limit the hours of "prerecorded" airtime. "There weren't even disc jockeys then, per se," said Besman. "There were radio announcers. Program directors picked the records, and they bought their own records. I was the first guy in Detroit to take records to the stations and give them away. The first real disc jockey in Detroit was Ed McKenzie, known as Jack the Bell Boy. He had a program and chose his own records. When I brought in my race records, which were different even for him, he was reluctant to play them, but he'd at least screen them. He was afraid of them: maybe he'd squeeze in one in twenty on the air. But whatever he played would be popular. He was a red-hot jockey for a long time."

An organ instrumental of "You Can't Be True, Dear" and then "Peg O' My Heart" by the Harmonicats—"If anybody tells you what record is going to go big, they don't know nothing" —put Besman and his partner on easy street. They moved the company to a larger office on Woodward Avenue next to the Paradise Theater, which like New York's Apollo and Chicago's Regal featured movies and name black acts. The flow of musicians and enthusiastic audiences gave Besman the same idea that was inspiring Elmer Barbara. In 1948 Besman recorded Todd Rhodes, a local black bandleader who headlined the Sensation Club. The four-hour session was nearly used up with numerous unsatisfactory takes of the tune Besman planned as the "A"-side. With five minutes left he said, "Well, let's try a boogie." The band fell into a groove. Besman called the result "Bell Boy Boogie" and had it pressed for his own label, which he named Sensation after the club. McKenzie was of course flattered and made it his theme song. The record then did so well that Besman was able to lease it for national distribution to Vitacoustic, the company which had supplied him with "Peg O' My Heart." "After that people started coming in to me with dubs. About November, it was cold I know, John Lee Hooker walked in.

"He had on an old overcoat and was skinny as could be; about my age, I thought. I looked at his shoes—I could see holes in them. He had a dub he had made someplace, real lousy reproduction, it was called 'Sally Mae,' a blues. He wanted to record, he said. He had a speech impediment too, he stuttered, and I thought, 'My god, how can a man like that sing? I gotta see this, I'm gonna try it.' I said, 'I'll record you, but alone, nobody else.' The record he had brought in had piano and drums. I didn't like them. He played for me, and I thought he had possibilities, but I was puzzled."

Besman figured that in 1948 it would be tough to sell a bluesman playing solo guitar—that was old-fashioned. Band records had accustomed the blues audience to a fuller, larger sound. Yet he also intuited that Hooker sounded best alone. "I knew I had to do something. So first we amplified his guitar. He had an old Stella and no amp. We put a mike onto his guitar, and we put a speaker—this was a tiny two-room studio, remember—we put it in a toilet bowl next-door, actually in a toilet bowl. Then we put a mike under that so the sound would bounce off the water —I wanted an echo effect. Then the sound went back into a speaker in the studio, came out of that, and got picked up along with his voice. I put a board under his feet to make his tapping louder, and put a mike down there.

"We worked almost three hours on 'Sally Mae,' getting nowhere. So I thought, what the hell, why don't I have him do a boogie, Rhodes did so well with one. But Hooker didn't know how to play a boogie. I said, 'Play like Todd Rhodes does.' He couldn't do it. So I showed him on the piano, me showing John Lee Hooker how to boogie. Finally he got it, or part of it, a semblance of a boogie. 'Boogie Chillen' isn't really a boogie, but John Lee, he had enough originality that it was a big record."

"Boogie Chillen" was a big record; it sold several hundred thousand copies—an enormous sale for a blues record in 1948. Moved by distributors like Besman in Chicago, Philly, Memphis, and Oakland, and aired by disc jockeys like Jack the Bell Boy in New York, Nashville, Boston, and Cleveland, it was a hit. Hooker and Besman were able to follow it; they did many sessions after the first one, and sixteen records were released on the Sensation label over the next three years. All had solid sales. "John Lee never wrote *songs*," said Besman. "He was illiterate. He'd have a subject matter, or I'd suggest something, and he'd do something with it, making up the words as he went along. He never had a plan, so the same song always came out different. He could make a story out of anything. In reality he's a genius."

The records, now available on three magnificent LPs (also containing much material previously unreleased), are startling musical experiences. At mid-century they had a powerful impact; both Carl Perkins and Bo Diddley, youngsters then, remember distinctly how the Hooker-Besman recordings hit them. Not only were the songs odd—apparently structureless and repetitive—but the sound of the records was different. "I couldn't figure how he got those sounds," said Bo Diddley. Bo couldn't have been expected to intuit Besman's ingenious echo chamber, but he did sense that the records had opened a new direction for music, one that he did much to expand a few years later.

"One night I was layin' down," sang John Lee. "Heard poppa and momma talkin', heard poppa tell momma, 'Let that boy boogie-woogie, he's a man now, let him have his fun.'" The music of John Lee Hooker is not like the music that most Americans were used to in 1948. It does not come back on itself, move in a cyclical pattern of verses and choruses, themes, or chord changes. It goes straight forward without deviation and, though it sometimes stops, never comes to a resolved end. Hooker creates it as he plays it; what get called songs are rhythms with which he associates particular words and keys. "I mostly play one chord, E or A. 'Boogie Chillen' I did in A, 'Hobo Blues' in A, 'Crawlin' King Snake' in A, 'In the Mood' in E. I hit that one chord most of the time, every once in a while hit something different for the change. Now I *can* do straight blues, twelve bars and three chords, but I don't like it. When I play it, I feel it taking something from me. It ain't me, it ain't John Lee Hooker."

He grinned. "I remember watching Willie Moore. I wanted to do like he did and have never wanted to do anything different. People tell me to change my style—it goes in one ear comes out the other. If I started doing something else, I'd hang it up first. I love my blues."

To make music without chord changes sounds easy, and in a way it is. With a guitar in standard tuning, hit the E chord and its variations in rhythms to your liking while you make up words to say how good or bad you feel, and you've started. John Lee Hooker creates overwhelming music by giving himself up, body and soul, to the idea implicit in making music that way: that music and time are synonymous. Two of his recent album titles express the point: *Endless Boogie* and *Never Get Out of These Blues Alive*. His music unfolds as his life unfolds, ever new and the same. Hooker stands at no distance from his music because he does not divide its time from his own.

Music and time—each have so many faces. A piece of music takes a length of time to play; its time is the grouping of its beats; its tempo is the relation of those beats to some normative time—beats per minute or "walking pace." A piece can be conceived of at one time, written at another, rehearsed at another, and finally performed at a scheduled moment in time. But those who make the music do not stand somewhere outside of time, able to hear the ticking of the metronome or clock but deaf to their own pulse. Neither music nor time come in pieces; "now" is always here. A musician is absorbed in each gesture as he makes it. He listens with the intensity of a stalking cat. John Lee Hooker sounds like doom stepping across the strings.

"Felt so good, kept on going my way—oooh, jump, jump, JUMP." One foot slaps the floor, light, dead even—bap bap bap. Hooker's foot seldom stops while he plays. After a while it is hard to hear: it becomes the silent rock against which all his other rhythms play. At moments his guitar is the drone of a single open string, then it becomes clanging full chords punctuated by fierce single-note runs in the upper registers or by subtle sliding walks down in the bass. Notes curl, bend, waver, and drop shimmering into bottomless wells. Silence and sound attack each other. "Strong statements which are full of surprises," wrote the late Al Wilson of Hooker's blues. It is true; you can not tell what is coming next with Hooker. Textures succeed textures, all different, all expressive; together they create one relentless drive forward, yet each is a spontaneous burst. Nothing seems premeditated—it is all inevitable.

"I had a nice-hearted woman, she was nice 'n' kind in her way deodeooooh oooh." Through it all rolls Hooker's voice, one of the most darkly commanding in blues. Its resonance comes from deep in his chest, and its bass is smooth as velvet, tough as leather. John Lee sings consciously, striving to make his voice as full as possible. He is proud of the results. "Yes, I like my voice," he said that Sunday afternoon at his kitchen table. "It's good. Sometimes I like to do ballads. I recorded two, 'I Cover the Waterfront' and 'Don't Look Back.' I have a voice for ballads though I sing the blues."

Besman didn't really teach John Lee how to boogie, but his imaginative engineering solved the problem he had seen. There was no way to record Hooker's immediacy; the contradiction was clear. The record itself had to be as immediate as Hooker. Hooker's job was to play, Besman's to make a sound image on sixteen-inch lacquer master discs. To charge that image he distorted and fractured Hooker's sound, emphasizing its discordances, putting its contrasts in sharpest relief, and accepting, even magnifying, its energy. Besman's records are expressionistic portraits of Hooker; in his hands the machinery which took sound and carved its image in plastic was no longer a ploddingly neutral tool for accurate reproduction, but a sensitively used medium for conveying transitory artistic gesture into permanence. "The engineering is astounding for its time," wrote Barrett Hansen, the erudite popular-record historian and disc jockey, who chose among Besman's masters for the two reissues on Specialty. Hansen noted the "power and presence of the guitar sound." "That's what I like, sound," said Besman.

The Hooker-Besman records make beautiful music today. They are not recordings of musical pieces but vivid fragments of a musical life. Through the recording medium we hear John Lee Hooker playing music as he advances in time. His willingness to accept instantaneous changes can be heard moment to moment. Hooker's music is fluid: uncrystallized by abstract conceptions of time, it passes through the medium with great force. Is recording, a medium of repetition, freed when its subject does not repeat? Is Hooker's time, his music, electrical, so true an expression of his nervous system that it is in sympathy with the medium which captures it? Or is the recording stylus, carving its spiral groove, a new pen for Hooker's language without letters?

Explanations are possible, but what matters musically is that the records are unique. They can be played over and over; the musical experience they present is always fresh. "My baby got something round like an apple, shaped like a pear, sure love to boogie, hey, hey, hey." Bap bap bap. "Ooooooooh!"

John Lee Hooker was not alone. In that migration north and cityward came a generation of bluesmen who were, as record jackets like to proclaim, giants. They had to be. With their fellow migrants, they needed great resources simply to survive. In the city, family and church were not so strong; the land and tradition had been left behind. To make music of city life required imagination and indomitability. The old themes of the blues could be reworked to express new dimensions of dislocation, but the sound and pace of country blues fit the city no better than brogans and bib overalls. A man played a guitar with the low accompaniment of crickets and whippoorwills back in the Delta; Detroit and Chicago never stopped their roar. How to make sounds which could stab through that noise with the same intensity that country blues had in its setting was a musical problem that many bluesmen new to the city encountered mid-career. They had to solve it to continue to make sense as artists and to get work as musicians.

The answer was electricity in all available forms. The electrifying of the blues guitar was the most dramatic change. Guitars had been electrified in the early 1930s. Among the first users of these electric instruments were slide guitarists in Hawaiian and country bands. In the late 1930s and early 1940s, amplified guitars became popular among lead and rhythm guitarists in country music, and some guitarists in large jazz bands went softly electric. These guitars were the first commonly available electrical musical instruments, and the pickers who played them were pioneers. The muted swoops and moans of Hawaiian and country bands had been dramatic; even more exciting was the brilliance of jazzman Charlie Christian.

The bluesmen, however, wrote the book. "You had to play electric in those clubs, they were so noisy," Hooker recalled, "but the sounds you could make! I loved electricity. You barely have to touch the guitar, and the sound comes out so silky. Electric sound is so lovely. I felt drawn into it. It's the feel of it, the touch of it. T-Bone Walker, he was the cat we all listened to for electric." Walker, a gnomelike Texan, drew notes from his amplifier which would hang in the air, glistening and tremulous, sending shivers through his audiences. His biggest hit, "Stormy Monday," says that though the days have different names, one is no better than the next. Lowell Fulsom learned from Walker, so did B. B. King and Albert King. Muddy Waters had learned from Robert Johnson, Son House, and Charley Patton; he added his own hooded fierceness, and made it electric in Chicago. His band—over the years there have been several bands—became the prototypical city blues band to which electricity was indispensable. Guitar, bass, and often piano were electric; vocals came loud through a public-address system. Waters' harmonica player, the late "Little Walter" Jacobs, played his harp directly into a microphone, creating sounds which are still haunting on record. Howlin' Wolf—a complete original. His personality is engraved on his records as indelibly as are those of the Parisian stonecutters on the gargoyles of Notre Dame. Elmore James, J. B. Lenoir, J. B. Hutto, Arthur Crudup, the incomparably magnificent Sonny Boy Williamson on amplified harmonica—these men and others, and their accompanying drummers, bassists, pianists, and singers, created electric blues in the late 1940s and early 1950s. Chicago was the center of the movement, and records produced by Leonard and Phil Chess document it well, but it happened in Memphis, Houston, Los Angeles, Oakland, and Detroit, and on the Sun, Aladdin, Specialty, Modern, Kent, Black and White, Aristocrat, Excelsior, and VeeJay labels, plus numerous others.

Some of these artists are dead or have stopped gigging; others, now in their fifties or sixties, are, like Hooker, performing regularly. Some, like Oakland's L. C. "Rockin'" Robinson, who works daytimes in a laundry, play only part time. Years of grooving have worn their styles into highly individual forms. To hear Lightning Hopkins today, playing solo electric backed by a drummer—philosopher and storyteller, darkly comic—is to hear a man steeped for many years in his single vision. "WOOOOOOOOOOOO, Mr. Charley, your old rollin' mill is burning down": the homeless little boy is still singing his awful news, and Mr. Charley still doesn't care. Jimmy Reed's rhythm is the beat of his songs and the maturing tempo of a lifetime spent playing the same music. His work is dense like a good farmer's earth. Like Hooker, Wolf, and the rest, he has been impervious to change while adaptable to endless modification.

"I like blues records," said one who digs them, "because even after you wear out the grooves, they still sound the same." The early electric blues records sound good today. The Chess bluesmen insisted that all the electrical distortions they knew in the clubs be left in during recording. The unpredictability of electrical sound—sudden crackles, hums, and changes of intensity in upper and lower registers—was much of its attraction. Little Walter was a master of pushing the electric sound system to its limits and beyond, making music of what was conventionally thought to be abuse of the medium.

The first electric blues were compact and dynamic. While jazzmen were breaking new ground rhythmically and harmonically, the electric bluesmen deviated little from a heavy four-quarter time and the twelve-bar form. But their creations, especially those for record, were sound images of compelling drama. Lowell Fulsom's "Tolling Bells" is a sombre masterpiece to which no stylistic title applies.

The point of the music was the communication of personality.

Each performer was determined to get himself, every wart in focus, across to his listeners. Sonny Boy Williamson fans don't disagree about what their man is saying: Sonny Boy laid it down, and there is no room for argument. To hear him is to know a man through his music. "Can't you hear me crying," shouts Wolf. I can. Was it the electricity or the power of their personalities that made the bluesmen's art so arresting? These men joined the two. They cannot now be divided.

In 1952 Bernard Besman left Detroit and the record business; he went to Los Angeles to sell paint-by-number kits in the eleven western states. He did a booming business and did not look back. His departure mattered little to Hooker then, though they are still friendly today. "Bernard, isn't he selling Bozo the Clown now?" said John Lee, his eyes twinkling. "Bozo the Clown!" When he couldn't record with Besman, he recorded elsewhere. Many musicians have played under pseudonyms to hide their moonlighting, but John Lee Hooker must have set a record. His discography is a mélange of names—from John Booker to Texas Slim—and labels—VeeJay, Chess, and Modern, and others whose names only collectors remember. While he was working with Besman, he also did sessions with Detroit's Joseph Von Battle, one of the first black record producers, who put Hooker on his own JVB label (years later he was the first to record Aretha Franklin).

"I was after the big bread," Hooker said. "I didn't care what they called me, or who they were—if they'd pay me, I'd play. I never changed my style, but I'd change my name." He didn't make big bread but did work steadily, an accomplishment in itself. National distribution of records and radio exposure gave bluesmen a national audience and a club circuit which they could work year round. Pay was bad, the hours were awful, and the distances, covered in overloaded sedans crisscrossing the South and city-hopping the North, were exhausting. A few bluesmen and women had made similar careers as far back as the 1920s, but they generally had the backing of the major record companies—Bessie Smith was on Columbia and subsidiary labels—or were under the aegis of booking agencies like the ill-famed TOBA, which treated its artists like valuable field hands. Hooker made his career on his own. Two decades earlier he, like his stepfather, would probably have had no career at all. He never kept a band together ("Too much work and trouble"), playing alone or, when the occasion, audience, or recording company demanded it, with pick-up ensembles. He was always an impressive stage performer. Besman remembered one early concert.

"I was his manager, sort of, for a while, and I got him on a show a radio man put together, a theater concert with about five different kinds of bands—swing, Dixieland, dance, something for everybody. He put John Lee on in the middle. He came out all by himself, sat down, and started playing. People didn't know what to make of him, whether to laugh, boo, or listen. After the first number, there was complete silence. Then John Lee started up again, a boogie, and people started tapping their feet. He had 'em then. By the end they were shouting."

In the late 1950s, however, work fell off. "Those were the hardest days," Hooker recalled. Like the other electric bluesmen (and jazz and country musicians), he found it hard to compete with the rhythm-and-blues and rock 'n' roll bands which after 1956 took the spotlight from all but the most popular performers. Hooker, Count Basie, and Frank Sinatra have lasted longer in show biz than many top acts of the 1950s, but rock 'n' roll as an entity, a musical form offering the novelty of constant change and the excitement of its own youth, swept all before it. Many R&B and rock artists had unique and forceful visions. They could cover current hits, get the kids by catching the beat of the latest dance step, and try to stay in favor by adding back-up singers, strings, or whatever gimmick was that month selling records. Many radio stations which had programed a wide variety of musics on many short shows went to rock around the clock. Ironically, the son of electric blues quickly and completely rose up over the father. The more famous Chuck Berry became, the harder a time Muddy Waters had getting heard.

A core of loyal blues fans, however, made it worthwhile for Hooker to continue touring and recording. Rock 'n' roll, the LP and the 45 rpm record, and the prosperity of the 1950s vastly increased the record-buying market. The bluesmen had gained overall, but in the new scene of 1960 Hooker and his contemporaries held about the same position bluesmen had held in the 1930s—marginal but profitable enough for those who specialized in it. "We were doing our thing," Hooker remembered, "but nothing was happening." The breakthrough days were a decade behind him, and he and the others faced years of gigging in the same clubs, to crowds growing old with them.

Suddenly a new and unexpected avenue opened in the early 1960s: folk music. The name as used by its earnest adherents meant nothing specific in terms of musical style. Old ballads, new ballads, "protest" and "message" songs, blues, and hillbilly; Mahalia Jackson, Doc Watson, and Lonnie Donegan; toothless old men, long-haired girls, and clean-cut boys in ice-cream striped buttondown shirts—it was folk music if you could sell it as that. What made a folk music fan a "folkie" was as much a distaste for music he considered not genuine as a love of "authentic" music. Confusion ensues when music is judged on nonmusical grounds, and the folk movement was so awash with scholastic and social politics that it seems lucky that anything of musical value emerged from it at all.

One thing that folk fans did agree on was that electric music was not folk music. At one concert in Boston a folk trio refused to share the bill with Bo Diddley. Doc Watson, who had played "Blue Suede Shoes" for years in an electric pop-and-country-rock group, was discovered as a "real" mountain musician. The reaction against electric music made no consistent sense: kids with new Harmony guitars copped every lick they could from records, all performers used microphones, and the folk movement spread through radio and records. The movement, however, did express a belated realization of how electricity had changed musical values. The search for "authenticity" and music with an old-time flavor (pre–World War II was ancient history) led few to music any more genuine than the sweet funk of the Orlons, who were then topping the charts with "Where do all the hippies meet? South Street, South Street," but it did

show that in the 1960s to find popular music that pretended to or did maintain preelectrical standards, you had to hunt for it.

Hunt the folkies did, and they came up with some winners. Son House, Mississippi John Hurt, Skip James, Elizabeth Cotton, Big Joe Williams, plus fiddlers a plenty, were found and put on stages, many of them for the first time in years. Most were remembered only because they had once been successful enough to record. Hooker was one of the "folk blues" discoveries. He played on a bill at New York's Gerde's Folk City with Bob Dylan when that bluesman was starting out. On the folk circuit—where Van Morrison traveled with him often—he played acoustic guitar alone, something he had not done in years. He enjoyed it. The folk fans were slavishly attentive, and he felt a kinship with the young musicians learning the blues. In Europe, where he had many followers, he was more likely to play electric. "Yes, I have been to England many times," he said, aware of the honor of it.

The later 1960s brought him even more recognition as the antielectricity argument became clearly untenable. Few rock or blues bands did his songs as they did those of Willie Dixon, Muddy Waters, and Elmore James, because Hooker's material defied copying. Many bands did the one-chord endless boogie their own way, and one, Canned Heat, made John Lee their personal Buddha of the blues. With him they recorded several excellent LPs which had huge sales, in the new market perhaps equivalent to the success of "Boogie Chillen." Singer Bob "Bear" Hite of the group edited the United Artists rerelease of Besman masters, entitled *Anywhere, Anytime, Anyplace.* By the early 1970s Hooker was finally making "big bread," and he moved from the flatlands of Oakland to the green suburban hills which overlook the whole sweep of San Francisco Bay.

There is now an audience which expects albums from him as they expect them from other established artists in the medium. Hooker's most recent discs have featured jams with young guitarists. He lets the others do most of the playing, but when he lets his guitar speak, there is nothing else to listen to. A musical conversation with "my old friend Van" Morrison was taped at the Lion's Share, a California club, for record release. Hooker, thin, black, and smiling, teased at his electric guitar as Morrison, chunky, red blond, and serious, worked out on a twelve-string. They discussed the state of the world today. It's a hard old world, they agreed, had been that way for a long, long time. What lay ahead? Morrison said nothing was gonna change: young people today may look different, but that isn't enough. John Lee, beaming affection for his junior colleague, held out hope for a time when the old folks had moved along.

Any of John Lee Hooker's recent recordings or the Hooker-Besman reissues are an excellent introduction to his art. The complete discography is vast and not widely available. Chess has issued an LP, *The Real Folk Blues* of material produced by Ralph Bass. It includes Hooker's foghorn version of "Waterfront." "The blues ain't nothing but what you feel," wrote Bass in his liner notes. "Don't count no bars, don't get 'teck,' just listen to what the man says." For VeeJay, Hooker recorded as an R&B singer, with a chorus and band. The songs are closer to standard blues than most of his work, and the full instrumentation is less stark a foil than silence, but Hooker comes through like gangbusters.

"Birmingham Blues" is a favorite of mine. He did it after the bombing in 1963 of the church in Birmingham, Alabama, in which four black children were killed. "I like to comment on what is happening in the world," Hooker said. "Maybe what I say about myself can help people with their problems." Many rushed to Birmingham to bear witness to their own horror; John Lee was more cautious. The band lays down a solid twelve-bar groove. Hooker sings, "I ain't going to Birmingham by myself." He repeats that, then his fear gives way to anger. "Take me an airplane, fly over Birmingham, drop me a bomb, keep on flyin' on." Anger changes to sadness: "Feel so bad when I read about Birmingham." In his confusion one thing is clear: "A man is just a man, God made this man, . . . God made everybody equal." Yet, "I don't know why Birmingham treat people the way they do." No, he says again, he won't go to Birmingham by himself, but "one day, Birmingham, Mississippi, Georgia, Tennessee, Kentucky, all those states, Arkansas, will fall in line." The song fades to nothing.

The Montclair Community Center, a small stone building in a pretty park, is a focal point for the neighborhood where John Lee Hooker lives, and a hang-out for local teenagers. Tonight he's agreed to play to open a series of Saturday-night concerts. The room is filled and smoky; the girls selling Kool-Aid flirt with everybody. Blue and pink lights are the only illumination, and though the average age of the crowd is sixteen, it feels like the funkiest blues dive in the world. A local band, recently disbanded but reassembled for tonight, is on first. They—a Chicano guitar player, black bassist, and white drummer—play breath-takingly fast. The guitarist is all over his axe. After five songs there is a certain sameness to their approach. They get a rousing hand as they go off.

A wait for Hooker. Finally the members of his Coast-to-Coast Blues Band are plugged in and ready. As usual they play several numbers without their leader. The two guitarists play fast and loud, packing in the notes and weird effects, splashing sounds on a crowd already drenched. Eventually John Lee steps to the center and sits in the chair waiting for him. He picks up the guitar and checks the tuning. His foot slaps the floor four times; a blues begins, slow and steady. He does not survey the crowd, he stares as if sightless straight out into the darkness. His left hand stays rooted in one spot at the top of the neck; his right, without a pick, floats over the strings. Mostly he rubs at them with the meat of his thumb. Sometimes he pulls upward with his index finger, and then he slaps all of them with his palm.

He sings. It is hard to make out the words. He loves a girl but she won't stay. Her name is Stella Mae. The band plays as before but considerably more subdued. They watch Hooker for clues; if he gives any, they are invisible. Suddenly he stops playing entirely, letting his hands hang limp. His foot doesn't stop, neither does the power of his presence. His singing is even and resonant. "Oh, baby, why did you have to go?" Then, almost before the action can be seen, his left hand has darted up the neck and a bolt of sound—twisted, searing, awful—travels through the room and is gone. Again silence from him except for the beating foot. The band continues until he raises his left hand, then drops it. End.

For an hour and a half this goes on. The tempos vary, but nothing is as frantic as it was before John Lee came on. The audience is spellbound. Hooker smiles occasionally, is more often meditative. The hour grows late, not too late for one more. He beats out a tempo, a bit faster this time. His guitar gets the song going, then he stops playing again. He puts the guitar down and stands up. He takes the microphone from its stand and moves to the edge of the stage. "Now momma said to poppa, 'I don't want that boy to boogie-woogie, when I was his age we didn't stay out all night doing the boogie.' And poppa said to momma, 'You let him boogie-woogie, he's a man now, let him have his fun.' "

"I'm fifty," John Lee had told me a few days before. He said it with a trace of ruefulness but also with a loose grin that made us equals. Now he is standing and dancing, his skinny legs shaking, his right hand slapping his thigh. "Oh I felt so good, went out and boogied all night long, love to boogie-woogie." The crowd dances with him, the spell complete. "Yes I love to do the boogie." John Lee's body waves back and forth as loose as a baby's. "Love to do the boogie, get up and do the boogie." Dance and sound are one thing. The room smells of fresh sweat. "Never stop the boogie, hey, hey, hey." The small red lights of the amplifiers shine like eyes. "Gotta do the boogie, oh, oh, oh yeah!"

Sometime it is over. The band starts packing up the equipment. John Lee Hooker steps off the stage and starts chatting with some friends. The exhausted kids trooping out into the night don't notice him.

● Are records music?

One whose ideas on music were formed before the 1950s would, I think, tend to answer no. When records were twenty-five years younger than they are today, heavy, thick, and breakable, played with steel needles kept in a dish beside the turntable, they were more likely to be considered an entertainment and a useful innovation than transubstantiated incorporations

ARE RECORDS MUSIC?

of the Muse. At least one eminent writer on music, Roger Sessions, has said about records that they are not, and cannot be, music. Sessions, a composer in the modern-classical tradition, is worth quoting at length:

> In music each moment is fleeting; it passes and cannot be completely recaptured, even through mechanical reproduction, which after all is imperfect simply through the fact of being mechanical. . . .
>
> Music, just because it is an art in which time and movement are the basic elements, needs constant renewal. This principle is extremely difficult to formularize and is full of pitfalls; but it is none the less real for that reason. Perhaps we can understand it most clearly if we consider a certain inherent limitation of that most useful instrument, the gramophone. I need not dwell on the fact of its usefulness, nor expatiate on the incredible advantages won through its invention and development. Any musician could add to the list of those advantages; and we of the mid-twentieth century are acquainted enough with the ordinary facts of technology to take it for granted that purely technical limitations can be either ignored or overcome. We may be sure that machines will be constantly improved and that reproductions will be constantly perfected. But what will never be overcome are the diminishing returns inherent in mechanical reproduction as such. We can listen to a recording and derive a maximum of pleasure from it just as long as it remains to a degree unfamiliar. It ceases to have interest for us, however, the instant we become aware of the fact of literal repetition, of mechanical reproduction—when we know and can anticipate exactly how a given phrase is going to be modeled, exactly how long a given fermata is to be held, exactly what quality of accent or articulation, of acceleration or retard, will occur at a given moment. When the music ceases to be fresh for us in this sense, it ceases to be alive, and we can say in the most real sense that it ceases to be music.*

*The Musical Experience of Composer, Performer, Listener,* by Roger Sessions

Music, for Sessions, is a most refined and sensitive means of expression through physical gesture. Mozart's vision lives not on paper or in any stored forms, but in the life of every musician who perceives and reexpresses that vision in his own way. The joy of music is constant recreation; though eternal, music does not keep. John Cage, of the modern-classical avant-garde, makes much the same point from a different angle: "Let no one imagine," he wrote in *Silence*, "that in owning a recording he has the music."

Those of us who came to musical consciousness in the 1950s accept records as music. We have, to be sure, unsorted attitudes and prejudices about music live versus music on record and about records as an art form. A "live" record is a recording of a concert, but the only record we'd call dead is one we don't like. "Overproduction" is considered a peril, but we are fully used to the most sophisticated techniques. In the end we'd say records are music not because we can prove the contention (as if anybody could prove or disprove it), but because we *believe* they are music. Little Richard's "Ready Teddy" is still a musical experience for me the thousandth time around. I still don't know how he does it. Since I believe my experiences are real, I believe records are music.

Sessions and Cage rest their arguments on musical traditions that go back to prehistory; the electronic storage of sound is only decades old. I know too that the simple E-A-B⁷ songs I strum in my room today are as alive in their moment as mechanical memories of virtuosity done years ago. Is there an unsolvable paradox here? To me the problem seems more like a confusion of terms and ideas natural in a time of musical change as profound as total upheaval.

What we call a record is a disc of plastic engraved with a spiral. Its inventors dubbed it "record" because that name seemed to suggest their brainchild's chief function. A sound could happen, you could capture it and hear it later; the disc was a "record" of an event. As with movie film (another plastic spiral invented about the same time), the scientific precision of the recording-reproduction process was thrilling. The gramophone's creators saw the machine as a logical extension of the joys of the Industrial Revolution—the discs themselves could be duplicated as easily as the sounds. The phonograph also seemed capable of providing an objective proof of the independent reality of particular events: you could leave the machine in the woods to hear the philosophers' tree fall; on the disc would appear a "record" of the fall that could validate the fall as real —even though nobody had heard the "actual" fall. Records were so real, RCA Victor's logo implied, they could fool a dog. The microphone, like the camera, could not lie.

What people most wanted honest pictures of, it turned out, was themselves. As with film, the most popular subject for exact reproduction and "moment recording" was people. The man who loved horses and bought still-life and landscape paintings did not often want abstract fantasies or animal sounds on film or disc. He wanted human stuff, and on records he wanted almost exclusively people making music. All the different people, therefore, who made the music of the early twentieth century started to appear on record. In the main, musicians were assembled in a room where they played as they usually played (subject to minor adjustments for studio purposes). The microphone was present as an extra and mechanical ear, overhearing everything. The sounds became squiggles on the spiral; the product was sold as a record. A new economic factor had entered professional music, and a new entertainment entered countless homes. Had music changed? For Sessions, writing in 1949, the answer was no. Records were "useful," particularly in teaching and in bringing music to those who otherwise would have listened little. Cage and others, sometimes dramatically, began to use tape and recording devices in their music, but they were still musicians who gave performances. They did not feel that a recording of their work could encompass it wholly.

In fact, and as usual, music was changing; the history of music can, ultimately, only be the story of what musicians and music lovers do. Increasingly audiences were willing to accept records as musical experiences which could satisfactorily substitute for live performance, and the Musicians Union started losing its battles to keep theater, hotel, restaurant, and party musicians in steady gigs. Despite union-inspired "recording bans," record making was a steadily expanding business, and more and more musicians gravitated to the studios as places of employment and expression. Long before 1950 cutting records had become an important facet in the career of professional musicians; some were specializing in it. The nearly simultaneous introduction in the late forties of the tape recorder, "high fidelity," the LP, and the 45 rpm disc boosted the importance of recording tremendously and opened up new possibilities. The cheapness, durability, and better quality of the new records brought many new listeners, and tape in the studio made possible wholesale editing and free rearrangement of the recorded sounds before their impression on vinyl. In the early fifties recording was almost reinvented—as it had been in the twenties when the early "acoustic" recording gave way to the electric microphone.

My own first inkling of serious editing was a Buck Clayton *Jam Session* record produced by George Avakian; it featured side-long improvisations by a brilliant ensemble of former members of the Count Basie band. The point of the sessions was to use the new time length of the LP to let the jazzmen cook on record as they could in clubs. But as Avakian's excellent and detailed notes made clear, the "Hucklebuck" I heard was really stitched together from two versions done in the studio. What came first had been played second—that can't be done in any club. That news was mildly upsetting, but it did not diminish my digging the record because I couldn't *hear* the difference. Hearing is always the paramount sense in appreciating music; it is the only sense used to comprehend a record.

On record music is solely an aural experience. All records

look, smell, feel, and taste alike. We all dig the covers and can recognize labels, but there isn't much to do with a record but listen to it. And just because records seem, no matter how bad, to be works of art, most people are a bit superstitious about using them for other purposes, throwing them away, or mutilating them. Turntables spin for good records and poor ones; the speakers, even when broadcasting, are motionless and mute. We listen blind. At a concert the appeal is to all our senses; on record music is pure sound. Alan Lomax, in the notes for his Southern Musical Heritage Series of records, makes the point with devastating understatement: "[On record] primitive voices answer symphonies; country orchestras reply to cool jazz on an equal acoustical footing." "Equal acoustical footing"—precisely: records abolish from musical consideration all factors except the quality and interest of the sounds heard. That makes it hard to fool the public with visual jive and cultural pretension. "It's what's in the grooves that count," is the motto of Gordy Records, a Motown company. Records made the whole world a cutting session for musicians of every bag, and no amount of double talk about Art could save the cats who could not blow. ("If you can't get it on the platter, cool your chatter," the saying goes.)

To recap: a record holds a moment of sound suspended forever, isolated from its association with the other senses. A record can record any sound, and the sounds recorded can be arranged in any way—reversed or sandwiched in time, changed in amplitude and duration. The method of recording is as "artificial" as that of film making, yet records, like film, have the strangely convincing "reality" of technologically perfect reproduction. So far, in its popularly available form, people have used the medium mostly to record music. Until the late 1940s records by and large recorded music passively—the microphone supposedly a neutral ear at a musical event which was essentially no different from the event at which no mike happened to be present.

Both Sessions and Cage divide what a record is (a plastic disc) from what it does (record sound). What you go to the store and buy is engraved plastic. That is what you get from the artist. You don't buy sound; you make the sound yourself by putting the plastic on the correct machine in the right way and turning on the electric current. Everything that goes on in the studio ends up, not as sound, but as wiggles on plastic which have, under the right conditions, sound correlations. Those wiggles are the music.

In short, a phonograph disc is plastic sculpture, and the music is the thing itself. The artist who makes a record scribes upon it his line, a line as readable and unique as the line of Matisse or Michelangelo. Unlike most sculpture (or painting), the appeal of record sculpture is not visual. You can see the brush stroke of Van Gogh and the spattered colors of Jackson Pollock; you cannot see, aesthetically, the line Chuck Berry creates on his discs (that is, you can't see the difference between his line and that of any other "recording artist"); you *hear* his line. In one sense you see it: the way Helen Keller saw. The needle, your agent as mechanical finger, "sees" the groove because it has a superb sense of touch. Remember doing it with your fingernail?

So the question really is, not can recorded sound be music, but can music be tactile, be stuff? Have records made music one of the plastic arts?

Yes, I think they have. That does not mean all recorded music is successful musical sculpture. Because recording *is* a true medium, it has particular demands and inherent laws; to use it to significant effect, the artist must learn what they are. That takes time: it's not uncommon for a technique to be invented, even used extensively, before the breakthrough comes that establishes it as an art. Part of that breakthrough is conceptual: if you think of records as recordings of events and therefore "less real" than the events themselves, then the records you make will probably sound that way. So if, as is likely, Sessions was thinking of classical records made before 1949, I would not dispute his judgment. Many of them are excellent "records,"

records of performances and personalities we are lucky to have; wouldn't it be nice to have records of Beethoven improvising? Contrasted with the drama of a classical concert—the workshop bustle of an orchestra tuning up, the hush as the lights dim— they may not satisfactorily deliver musical experience.

All recordings of music may not be music, but all records do record. Whether or not the Beatles' *Sgt. Pepper's Lonely Hearts Club Band* is music, it is a record of the event, the release of the *Sgt. Pepper* album, whose striking sounds and cover instantly fascinated millions, in the spring of 1967. This is why popularity is important to the art of recording; if a record is influential at a point in time, it then becomes a "record" of itself as a historical moment. Unlike a recording of a performance, which serves only as a reminder of an event (as historical documents only suggest the past), the record *Sgt. Pepper* is a complete record of *Sgt. Pepper* as event.

All records may not make it as sculpture, but there is no reason why music cannot be a plastic art. All art comes down to physical movement; whether you write, dance, or play the saw, you are moving your body in gestures capable of communicating meaning to other humans. It is all body language. Keats wanted to find out how Shakespeare sat as he wrote. In the plastic arts the aim is to trace those gestures onto stuff so that even though the gesture itself disappears with its completion, a clear enough "record" of the gesture remains for people to be able to comprehend its meaning. If this can be done successfully on paper, stone, bark, cave walls, clay, and canvas, it ought to be possible on vinyl. If painting had originally been the artist standing in the dark and waving glowing embers, would it have made sense to say that similar gestures were not painting when caught on a surface?

Nor, I think, can a fundamental distinction be made between tracings left by sound and tracings left by a chisel. Sound directs a carving stylus; there is a transfer of energy: as the stylus moves, matter is molded in characteristic forms. The body movements of all arts make sounds—just the sounds which

Cage calls silence ("unintended indeterminate noise") and from which he builds his music; it is the sonic frequencies generated by the chisel's impact that split a sculptor's stone.

If music can be made plastic, yet not all music recorded is music on record, which records are music and which are not? I will not say a record you hold dear as a triumph of musical expression is not music, only a record of a musical event. If you think it music, it is music for you. I can suggest some generic distinctions, but I won't fight over any of them.

First, I think it likely that the use of electrical instruments in the music recorded makes a substantial difference to the musicality of the result. The added "something" that electrification undeniably brings to instruments may more vitally charge the scribing needle, itself an electric instrument.

Second is intention: for a musician to become a successful sculptor in plastic he must want to be one. Musicians who actively seek out opportunities to record, who take the time to learn the unique characteristics of the medium, and who believe that records are central to their art are more likely to make musical records than musicians for whom recording is a peripheral activity. It is not enough to let the microphone "overhear" you at work, you must work with the microphone.

Third, music strongly expressive of personality, music that is human in a bold and forthright way, dedicated to immediate communication, comes off well on record. Decisive and vigorous gestures are needed to mold the resisting vinyl in wiggles that will excite listeners. "You can't show a man thinking," Alfred Hitchcock has said about film. Records, like film, capture action best. This is what people prefer; in these new and near-perfect mirrors we most want to see ourselves, and the more vital the recorded image, the more vital the communication. Something *is* lost with storage, so it's best to put in more at the beginning; as with food, spicy stuff keeps its taste longer than bland.

To prejudice-blinded eyes rock 'n' roll musicians might not have looked like much back in 1954, a bunch of gaudy niggers and country boys whumping it up with their installment-plan Gibsons, but those rock 'n' rollers were ready, willing, and able at a watershed moment in musical history, and they seized it. They made music that could live as music on plastic; their "records" are not recordings of events long gone but are present musical material. The rock 'n' rollers used electric instruments without shyness: flamboyantly personal, even eccentric, showmanship was their bag, and the music and its name were brand new. From the start recording was a crucial part of their musical expression, in many cases the core of it. The growth of their music has gone hand in hand with the growth of the science and business of recording. Just as Beethoven demanded larger and larger pianos for his music, rock 'n' rollers, more than any other modern musicians, have demanded and used all the extensions and advances in recording.

The best test of the musicality of rock 'n' roll records is how people respond to them; the history of rock 'n' roll's first two decades is evidence for rock records' musical content. Rock 'n' roll records immediately assumed a special significance which records of other musics did not attain: the rock 'n' roll audience treated its records as musical experiences complete in themselves. Loving golden oldies is not "record collecting" in the pre-1950s sense. Rock 'n' roll records were never by-products. The records did not try to copy "live" music; live rock shows presented copies of records. The Hit Parade of the top ten songs became a Top 40 of supercharged records.

It is in large measure due to its success in establishing records as a true medium for music that rock 'n' roll has won an audience larger and more spontaneously responsive than any other music now commands. It is not that rock 'n' roll is "winning" over "weaker" musics, but it has, because of its success at musical communication, created tremendous interest in communication through music. Music is news today because this moment is significant in music's own history: it is the moment when music began to live over time as sculpture. Rock 'n' roll will stand.

I will make all this a particular tribute to Chuck Berry. If one person symbolizes this moment, I think he is the man. Had Charley Parker lived, he and jazz might have made their records sculpture. The reasons jazz didn't, as Ralph Gleason has pointed out, are that jazz did not take to electricity and that Parker did die. For a decade after Parker's death jazz retreated from the ideal of the extroverted personality. But Berry was building on electric blues, the music of the first musicians to use electric instruments without self-consciousness and with popular success. Moreover, Berry's artistic stance was fundamentally one of liberation from restraint, liberation both by anger and by joy. He eschewed irony and introverted fantasy for a boldness and aggressiveness previously unequaled among black American musicians. His music—three-minute songs as sharp as arrows—reached a huge and youthful white audience. They were at once enthralled.

His intuitive understanding of the importance of the music he was making, down to its last nuance, is staggering. Almost all his songs are about rock 'n' roll; some define it. His best records have not aged an instant; in fact, it is only with almost twenty years' perspective that I am able to get any conscious grasp on what blew my mind as I heard "Maybelline" night after night on the Bob Clayton show in 1955. The precision of Berry's gestures, the clarity of his musical ideas, the drive of his rhythm, and the exactitude of his lyrics become more impressive with each listening. His achievement as a musician and recording artist is monumental. Although racist persecution crimped his career, wounded his pride, and sapped his strength with two trials and a three-year prison sentence, Berry is the fourth great *B* of Western music. How do I know? Chuck told me so himself, and I believe him:

> Well, I'm gonna a write a little letter
> Gonna mail it to my local dj
> Yeah, an' it's a jumpin' little record
> I want my jockey to play,

Roll over Beethoven,
I gotta hear it again today.

You know my temperature is risin'
The juke box is blowin' a fuse,
My heart's beatin' rhythm,
My soul keeps a singin' the blues,
Roll over, Beethoven!
An' tell Tchaikovsky the news. . . .

Roll Over Beethoven!
Roll Over Beethoven!
Roll Over Beethoven!
Roll Over Beethoven!
Roll Over Beethoven!
An' dig these rhythm and blues!*

*Everything I know I taught myself.*
—Bo Diddley

● Bo Diddley, a protean genius and as great an artist as any who has graced American shores, lives in exile in California's San Fernando Valley. His house, a medium-to-large tan ranch-style, is on the 17500 block of a winding street in that suburban

nation. It is surrounded by cars. In front is the orange Dodge he bought for his wife's birthday because he had a lot of work in August. Beside it is a Ford LTD limousine he got cheap from a chauffeur service a few years ago. In the side drive are four more cars, all flashy Detroit numbers Bo salvaged from junkyards and then transformed. He works on them in his spare time (of which in exile he has a lot) to keep his mind off money worries and his hands busy. He could quit the music business any time—he's been threatening to for years—or he could lose a finger; in either case he hopes car work could be his living.

A big tree with small, shimmering leaves shades the house prettily. On the stoop beside the screen door, which hangs limp from countless bangings, are cases and cases of RC Cola empties. To the left, seen through a window, hangs a picture of Bo so big that only his glasses and one ear are visible. There are always kids on the stoop—one of Bo's own four or his two grandchildren, or almost any kid in the neighborhood: Bo's house is the hang-out for the whole block. Scattered underfoot are dozens of canceled checks; when Bo noticed them, he first said the hell with 'em, then figured he'd better clean them up because some might be important for business.

His exile is not complete, nor is it entirely bitter. Indeed, it could be said not to exist. Bo Diddley does play what jobs he can get; since 1970 he has made several LPs, including the magnificent *Black Gladiator*. Everybody calls him "the great Bo Diddley" and awards him place as a founder of rock 'n' roll. Yet in a perfectly simple way he is without honor in his own land. The return to him, in any form, has not been commensurate with what he's given, and he knows it. He wants what he deserves, but he's too proud to beg. So he's biding his time, looking for work and fixing up his cars.

In the kitchen his wife Kay, a tall and beautiful woman, is making dinner. Tan, Bo's oldest daughter, is helping; her husband, who works in a Valley styrofoam plant (night shift), and their two kids are in the living room, kept dark in the late afternoon for the TV. Walter Brennan is on in some crummy serial—another underrated artist doing time. Two white teenie-boppers from the block are watching from the sofa. Connie, who writes songs and plays rhythm guitar in Bo's band, is giving her chihuahua, Poopsie, a good scratch; Bambi, Kay's chihuahua, looks on jealously.

Spider, Bo's shaggy mutt, is asleep under the carved Japanese chair, and Bo himself is seated at the card table, half an eye on the tube, the other eye-and-a-half on the life around him. He's washed up from his day underneath the Chevy van, but he's still in a T-shirt and baggy corduroy jeans. Ricky McMillan, an old friend who is temporarily living in a room beside the studio out back, walks in with a stack of shrimp cocktails and some Slim Jim sausage sticks. Bo takes four of the shrimp tins for himself and orders one of the kids to put the Slim Jims beside his bed. The kid goes. Bo is Daddy in his house.

He digs into the shrimp methodically, from time to time scratching his chin with the plastic fork. It's tiny in his hands, which are huge and hooklike, cracked like a laborer's. His arms are thick beams, and his shoulders are rounded like the great Marciano's. Bo Diddley is a small black mountain, mobile but immovable. The peak is his hard, round head, and from it, through glistening glasses, beam eyes whose fire he can hood but never quench. When he laughs, his mouth falls way open, baring wide gaps between his teeth.

Bo shrugs. His shrimp are gone. Spider is nosing around the fake bonzai tree beside the fireplace. "Spider!" Bo calls, his voice booming with reproach. "What you doin', dog? Tammi, take Spider out before he pees all over it." Spider, as woebe-gone as ever I saw a dog, trails out in disgrace.

"Kay, d'you see what Spider tryin' to do? *Spider*, messing around that bush, hah, he know better than that."

Bo looks down his nose at tiny Poopsie, yapping at all the commotion. "*That* dog, hah! Hey, somebody throw that joker down the garbage disposal." He laughs at his own joke.

"As I was saying," he continues, "I started out doing my thing. I did my thing, am still doing my thing, and plan to keep doing my thing. But see, where I lost a lot of my stepping ground is right here: I had the doorknob in my hand. I opened the door —everybody's *gone*. Are you ready for that?" His eyes are burning.

Americans have often divided their response to creativity into two bags, one for Art and one for entertainment. Proud of their Art, they have enjoyed their entertainment not because all entertainment is art, but because the greatest artists in America have in their own times been considered entertainers. There are good writers, architects, and painters who have always been "taken seriously," but the bulk of the heavies have, like Raymond Chandler, Buster Keaton, and Jack Benny, been out there to please the people. Their art is the work they do. They either get paid for it or they don't. Their self-effacement tends to make their art invisible; their generosity puts their audience so at ease that the masses are quick to make the proffered gifts their own—and the admission fee means you don't have to say thank you. Those masses have been more beloved than loving; after their first and only honeymoon with success, many popular artists have had long struggles to keep alive the romance on which their livelihood and means of expression depended. Though famous, they have often been lonely, and their rewards have been so mixed with abuse that it's hard to tell them apart.

With these artists in popular media, Bo Diddley stands in the first rank. His lifework evidences a cohesive and profound vision, sustained by a confident personality and driven home with a power dark as voodoo. His values, drawn directly from his own life, are universally human, and he makes them convincing, even overpowering. A master of his craft, he has made major innovations within it. He is a fine musician, a singer of great gusto, and, rare indeed, a devoted teacher. He's more funky than primitive, and funky can be sophisticated too. Inadmissible fare for honky TV, he is too large a presence for the modern stage. Though the rock industry is not sure it wants him, the

*Bo and Kay with apple*

only art that can contain him today is rock 'n' roll music.

Rock 'n' roll music does not exist without electricity, but not all electric music is rock 'n' roll. As Sisyphus knew, to make a rock roll you gotta work at it. Rock 'n' roll energy comes from humans plugging away at existence, yet its pace is never trudging. From the first rock has had a feeling, an indelibly vivid something *more:* in the beat but more than the beat; that intensity that made nonbelievers call it noisy when played low and believers know it had to be played loud. That feeling came from a new emotional level. It was released by the discovery of the possibility of freedom. Nothing less than that could have made electricity its ally. Rock 'n' roll was black American liberation music (a tune quickly taken up by young whites); its creators were black heralds. Though there hadn't been much "progress," "Negroes" were recovering from the traumas of captivity and enslavement. Rock 'n' roll occurred at that moment in the healing when the patient, if not well, first gets back on his feet. More blacks had confidence in their own worth and were eager to assert it. The story of that attitude growing into a movement and then a revolution is as well known as rock 'n' roll's, and the two are clearly linked in parallel.

Even within the black musical tradition rock 'n' roll was a brash development. By the early 1950s, black musicians, though often in a favored position, had been only slightly more aggressive socially than black people at large. They stuck to their own and tried to please (or at least not to offend) when in the white world. Much truth was said in irony and understatement, but the involuted style and language of the 1940s bebop (a re-bop) movement was as outrageous as black musicians had dared get.

Rock 'n' roll stars were wild men. Their extravagant individualism reached and passed beyond the borders of conventional sanity. They wrote songs, all crisp and short, as up-to-date as their cars and flashy clothes. Technically their playing was less intricate than their jazz contemporaries and less subtle than their blues predecessors, but they had as compensation a genius for stagecraft. Their blues had a heavier beat and gaudier lyrics, and they went outside the blues to take ideas from pop, country, and gospel. They avoided "hard life" blues themes, concentrating instead on the joys of dancing; the sexual metaphors of the blues they extended into cocksure statements of total male potency. Their aim was to get the message of "feeling good" across by any means necessary—and they did.

Of the many black creators of rock 'n' roll, four stand preeminent: Little Richard, Fats Domino, Chuck Berry and Bo Diddley. Little Richard Penniman is an "ecstatic" more than an artist; what he does, by his own admission, is up to God more than to himself. Antoine "Fats" Domino's music rolls on as surely as the Mississippi through his native New Orleans. Chuck Berry, an angry and accurate prophet, makes rock 'n' roll about rock 'n' roll. Bo is their Prometheus. His songs are hymns to himself. Not that he is vain—the reverse—but he is one black boy who made twenty-one, and that is a discovery worth a thousand songs.

> *I'm a Man*
> *I spell it*
> *M, A, N,*
> *MAN*

Ellas McDaniel (Bo Diddley is a childhood nickname that stuck) was born on December 30, 1929, in Magnolia, Mississippi, which makes him nominally a Delta-born bluesman. But his mother, then only sixteen, moved downstate to McComb when Bo was a baby. He never saw his father, and after age six was raised not by his mother but by her cousin, Mrs. Gussie McDaniel, who took him with her children when she moved to Chicago in about 1934.

"My real mother is a high-spirited and wonderful woman," he said at the start of three days of talking about his life, "and I always dug that she couldn't raise me. About my father, I don't think he and my mother were ever really together. I never cried over not seeing him, but I do feel he could have been a man and come by once to say hi. Even if he didn't have nothing to give, just say hi. It would have been the greatest thing in the world.

"Know something? I'm classed as a Negro but I'm not: I'm what you call a black Frenchman, a Creole. All my people are from New Orleans, the bayou country. Just like Fats. French, African, Indian, all mixed up. I like gumbo, dig? Hot sauces, too. That's where my music come from, all the mixture. Some peoples are known for this, some for that. Mix 'em and it can get weird, hah!"

Listening to Bo was an experience; he'd talk in wide-ranging circles, pausing to fit great chunks of his philosophy in between the facts of his life, which he had little interest in organizing in sequential patterns. He could get serious about memories dear to him, but his chief attitude expressed the rough-and-ready logic of a man who keeps a wry eye on everything that's going down and isn't afraid to speak his mind. A few times he approached things he thought he shouldn't discuss, then he'd go ahead: "I'm not a person to lie about anything" was his explanation.

He remembers being lonely as a little boy—"I think that's why I like people around now"—but in Chicago there were plenty of cousins to play with on the sidewalks of the South Side around 47th and Drexel. Racially nothing had changed. "Where I was living, it was just like Mississippi. We could cross Drexel Boulevard and be in *trouble*. There was a mass stupid confusion goin' on all the time, and even as a child I called it what I call it now: stupid. I was never taught to hate people but 'Do unto others as you would have them do unto you.' That is beautiful.

"I got a paper route across Drexel, man. Me and my cousin. I was about twelve years old. We had made three or four deliveries the first day, and we had to cut it loose or get half *hung* over there. This is the way things were and I just couldn't see why people had to be this way."

Home was strict and proper. Bo wasn't supposed to leave the

block without permission; his uncle, who still works at a meat-packing plant, and his adopted mother were regular members of the Ebeneezer Baptist Church. Another uncle (his mother's brother) is the pastor of several churches in Biloxi, Mississippi, and Bo calls himself a religious man, "even though I play rock 'n' roll." But the Ebeneezer Baptist, with its big organ, robed choir, and Sunday school, was never his bag. When he was seven he made the mistake of saying one day that he wanted a violin like the man in church. His parents couldn't afford one, so the church scraped together thirty dollars and bought him one. That was his first instrument, and he labored at it, instructed by Professor O. W. Frederick, for twelve years. Today he remembers he played music by "those German guys, Heichhof or something, I could pronounce 'em when I was into it."

The music he yearned for was "down home." "I used to stand around and listen at the sanctified church. Break off from home and stand on the sidewalk and look in the door. Or they'd leave a window open and I'd climb on a milk crate and peep in at 'em dancing and shaking their tambourines, and I'd say, 'One day I'm gonna get me something that sounds like that.' A thing I used to hum was a thing they used to play all the time." To demonstrate, Bo turned to a piano, fiddled with it, then played a gospel chorus, the chords ascending, falling, going up to a climax, then falling back to rest. In them, partly disguised by the religious flavor, was the Bo Diddley beat. Chink-a-chink-chink, ca-chink-chink. Chink-a-chink-chink, ca-chink-chink. Steady as a rock. Bo turned back.

"And that always stuck with me. The Baptist church was all stately and calm, but in the sanctified church, everything was rockin'! This is where I got part of my rhythm; my music is really based around a religious beat."

He was thirteen when his half-sister gave him his first guitar, to the horror of his adopted mother. She wanted him to be a concert violinist, but for Bo the violin faded into the background, and by the time he was fifteen he and his guitar were out on the streetcorner with a cousin on washboard, picking up nickles and dimes. By that time he was out of school and had started boxing, then as important as music to him: a four-eyes had to look out for himself.

"I was trying to figure out about growing up and molding myself to manhood, and since I knew I had to walk this dirt road alone, I might as well learn not to be scared. Boxing was it. I was a light-heavy, one of those hard-hitting dudes, hah! Used to go to a neighborhood gym or over to Eddie Nichol's gym at 48th and Michigan. It wasn't that I wanted to be tough, but I think you should like something rough, to be a *man*. I figure 'man' means more than being male. Like the word 'woman.' What does a woman do? She bears children. This is something great, so she has a title: woman. *Man*, that's a *word*, looks like to me. 'Man' means to me a cat is supposed to protect himself as well as his family, put his life on the line for them. Having the opportunity to be a husband, father, and provider is a good title, if you live up to it."

By the time he was sixteen his streetcorner group had progressed to the point where it had a name, the Langley Avenue Jive Cats (sometimes it was the Hipsters): Roosevelt Jackson on washtub bass, Jerome Green on maracas, and Bo on guitar. Jerome, of "Bring It to Jerome" fame, joined by accident. "When I met Jerome, he was a jazz cat, played a tuba that was bigger than he was. One day when we had nothing to do I brought him some maracas and taught him how to shake 'em. I said, 'Hey, why don't you come down to the corner and pass the hat for us?' He said he couldn't; that was begging. Begging? Hah! It was *work*. But he came in his Buick—a real smoker, made five gallons to twenty blocks—and passed the hat, saw the dollars falling in, and asked me next day, 'Bo, when you gonna play that corner again?'

"We was then playing behind a cat named Samuel Johnson; he could sing like Billy Eckstine and he sanded, too," I looked blank. "Sanding? Oh, he was terrific. He'd carry a bag of sand around and a piece of board. We'd play 'Tea for Two' or something, and he'd get up on a board and do a thing, his feet gliding. That cat cracked up. I thought he was beautiful, but he was no Casanova-looking dude, and people telling him he was ugly broke him. Don't know what happened to him, but he was something else.

"Music I liked was Louis Jordan and Nat Cole. John Lee Hooker, too. I tried to catch his strange guitar sounds, but at first I couldn't understand him. My main man was Muddy Waters. He and Little Walter used to play at a place—man, I got throwed out of there enough times 'cause I was underage. They had a juke box near the door. I'd get in the corner between the juke and the cigarette machine, where I could split when I saw the man coming. One night I got slapped upside the head." But Muddy was only a few steps from playing on the street himself, and when Bo and the Jive Cats had a few tunes together, they started hustling for club dates.

"Man, we played some smoky holes, bars under the el station, in storefront clubs, and it was hard, so hard you was looking for the *worm* to pull the *robin* into the ground, you dig? You ask cats like Muddy and Willie Dixon and J. B. Lenoir, you ask 'em how hard it was to get five dollars or six dollars together on a weekend. When you worked a club you worked it. Sometimes I'd make less than I would on the street, because on the street they'd say, 'How cute that boy is,' and put in fifty cents; but in a club you had to have it together or be cut."

Blues couldn't pay the bills or even come close; off-stage, Bo was just one more black man looking for work. "I was on relief when my oldest daughter Tan was nine months old. I was with my first wife. I couldn't get a job noplace. I knew how to run a whole lot of different machines but no use. Back in 1951, '52, '53, I'm talking about. I went to get some welfare and I told the people my kid was hungry and sick *right now*, and they told me I had to make one more trip down there before I could get any money. What was I supposed to do—turn off a valve to stop her from crying because she was hungry? The next step was to stick somebody up, and I didn't want to do that.

"When a cat dedicated to his family gets so his hind parts is dragging and he can't get work—I have been this way. I ain't just sitting here talkin'. Every morning I'd get up and walk from my home on 47th Street down to 12th Street, trying to find a job. Get on the streetcar 'til the conductor saw me, then jump off and wait on the next one. I was looking for anything, plain labor, but you'd go into a place and they're talking thirty-five or forty cents an hour. That's no money; that's about twenty-nine dollars a week. Are you ready for that? You wouldn't believe it existed in the fifties but I worked on some of 'em. I unloaded boxcars, and then I drove dump trucks. Truck driving wasn't so bad, but there was discrimination against black drivers. I'd drive to the stone quarry and couldn't get no stone. Everybody was told a black dude's bad business; a black dude ain't even supposed to *be* there. I just told people, 'Hey, man, I'm a *man*. I don't give a damn what color I am, I didn't ask to come into this world no way.'

"If you got no money in this country, you is out of it. 'Land of the free and home of the brave'—hah! Ain't *nobody* free in America without money." When Bo gets talking about money he gets angry. With those who've worked a lifetime without ever feeling financially secure, he can become obsessed with money, licking wounds long open. He doesn't like to harp on the subject, but has decided not to avoid it. He does try to be fair. "One thing: a lot of black people don't want to see nothing but that they've been mistreated for three hundred fifty years or whatever it is they are screaming about, but there is whites who've been in as much hard luck as the black man. Down in Mississippi the only difference between us and some white folks was that they could go in the front door of a restaurant and sit down and eat, and the black cat had to go in the back and stand. But we was *all* scratching, you dig?"

In 1954 Bo was twenty-six; he had quit boxing because he saw no future in it except getting punchdrunk, and he was working regularly as a bluesman. He was still driving trucks, and when he made his first record it was not because he had plans of becoming a full-time professional. "I went in to Chess Records 'cause I finally realized it was right around the corner from where I lived. Went in, did my thing, signed a mess of papers, and went out feelin' no different. I heard I had a hit in a couple of weeks. Scared me to death; I didn't know what was happening. I had never been nowhere in my life, and they told me I'd have to go on the road.

"My first contract was for eight hundred dollars. Two nights in New Orleans, me and Howlin' Wolf on the same show. I had never seen eight hundred dollars in one pile in my life. I took off for New Orleans and got lost, taking the road for St. Louis instead. I played the job and made it back home with thirty-five cents. We had blowouts, breakdowns, tickets from the Southern police, in and out of jail once, and paying the musicians—oh, man, was I green, I didn't know nothing. But I went to school and I *learned*, man, the hard way. They graduated me—put me from kindergarten right through college!

"Then I quit driving, but it wasn't because of the record really. I was gonna quit anyway. A few months before, my daughter had been sick, and the boss told me that if I took a day off to take her to the hospital he'd make me take four days off without pay. So I did what he would have done if it had been his kid sick. I said, 'Crazy, you get the four days ready, 'cause I'm going.' 'You need a rest,' he said. Man, it was a bad scene for a black dude then.

"A while later I made the record. I walked up to him one day and said, 'Here's your keys, baby.' He looked at me and said, 'What's this?' 'I ain't going this morning,' I said. He says, 'Mac, did you make a record?' I said, 'Yeah, how you like it—pretty nice, huh?' He said, 'This record got anything to do with it?' I says, 'Not really, but remember the day you threatened me a few months ago? About how I needed a rest? Well, now I'm taking a rest, a long rest, man.' "

The record he had made was "Bo Diddley" backed with "I'm a Man," two roughly hewn self-portraits. "Bo Diddley" is in the form of an old folk round ("Daddy's gonna buy you a looking-glass. If that looking-glass should break," etc.). But Bo slips in a few jokes ("If that diamond ring don't shine, I'm gonna take it to a private eye. If that private eye can't see, he ain't gonna get that ring from me."), boasts of catching a bearcat, and floats out on a piece of nonsense—"Hey, Bo Diddley, have you heard, my pretty baby says she's a bird." Bo's beat is there, fully realized; he sets it with his guitar, and maracas and drums played like congas are its underpinning. That beat has often been described as "shave and a haircut, two bits," the joke rhythm you beep on your car horn at the drive-in. Nothing is further from the truth. Bo's beat is his own pulse made art. More than a signature, it is his ultimate statement, the stable matrix from which his music flows.

Yet the beat, four-quarter time shoved off center like the beat kept by the claves in West Indian music, is complex and changing. Bo can syncopate it any way he wants to. His physical strength makes it profoundly sensual, and the maracas evoke Africa or Haitian. The beat is dense, but its ambiguity of shadings opens it up and keeps it moving. It is the Bo Diddley beat: "Everybody from New Orleans," Louis Armstrong once said, "got that thing."

"I'm a Man" is a more standard blues, Bo's obvious tribute to his idol Muddy Waters and "Hootchie-Kootchie Man," a Willie Dixon blues that had become Waters' trademark. The difference between "Hootchie-Kootchie Man" and "I'm a Man" (and between Muddy and Bo) marks the difference between the blues and rock 'n' roll. Bo's song is a good imitation of Muddy until the refrain; then Bo sings "I'm a Man." Spelling out "man" to avoid any mistake, Bo rings the consonants like tolling bells. The refrain stands independent within the song; the sureness of its voicing makes the Muddy-style choruses that surround it, with their magic and exaggerations, seem boasting. But "Bo Diddley" was the A-side, the novelty hit which established Bo as a jokester, a "rock 'n' roller," less serious than the "bluesmen" who preceded him. "I'm a Man" expresses Bo's continuity with and development from the blues. Bo was a good pupil with good teachers. "We knew at the time there was a difference between me and Chuck on one hand, and Muddy and those cats on the other, but it wasn't no generation gap," said Bo. "We were just younger, that's all." "I dig Bo Diddley," said John Lee Hooker. "My favorite of his was that one, you know, 'I'm a Man.' Oh, man, that's a *strong* record."

"The same thing is true today with the cats that are younger than me," Bo went on. "But, man, I don't know what we're gonna do now that Jimi Hendrix copped out on us. He took my thing one step further. He was the only black cat who could play psychedelic."

At a break in talking on the first day, Bo gave me a tour of the house. "As you can see, I have a family, and we don't live fancy," he said. "I don't believe in living beyond my means." True enough: Bo's place is a family-worn home. In the breeze-way there are old toys, bikes with one wheel, and folded patio chairs. The pool is empty; Bo will sandblast it one day, but the kids use it for baseball. Past that is the cinderblock studio he built, a two-track job with a darkroom in one corner. It's mostly used as a rehearsal hall for the teenage bands Bo coaches for free. By the garage are scattered tools and a pile of sand left over from cement work.

Inside, the few decorator items like the carved Japanese chairs don't disrupt the calm of the wall-to-wall and the drapes. On a wall near the bathroom is a gold record for the "Outstanding Album Sales in 1962" of *Bo Diddley's a Gunslinger;* Bo paid for it himself. The kitchen door is the only door anybody uses, and the kitchen is the center of the house. It's Kay's room. Kay tries to stay out of Bo's public life because she knows some fans like to think of him as single and because she knows some people are prejudiced. Kay is white and from Georgia.

"The first time I met Ellas," she said, in a soft twang, "I drove two hundred fifty miles to see him and two hundred fifty miles back. He and Jackie Wilson were the only ones I'd drive that far to see. It was 1960. My girlfriend was going with a guy in the show, and before it started Bo sent her out with the message, 'Come to me.' I played it cool and said, 'He knows where to find me.' But later we went up to the dressing room. He was sitting there like King Tut, aiming at playing around, here tonight, gone tomorrow, like the rock 'n' roll star he was. But I had some money to follow him, and time—I wasn't doing anything else. He wasn't figuring on that. Tried to avoid me for a while, then he gave up."

Partners in business and song writing as well as family life, Bo and Kay get along well. The bedroom is their room, and they are proud of it. You enter to face a trellis covered with a jungle of plastic plants; all is dark until you get accustomed to the glow of indirect red lights along the ceiling. The long-tufted carpet is black and deep; the walls are black, too, and there are more plastic jungles along the baseboards. One wall is walk-in closets. At one end of it are Bo's old show clothes, including the few ruffled shirts left of the 175 he once owned. His guitar is in one corner. The center of the room is a low platform, also carpeted, and in the center of that is a king-size mattress covered with comforters and colored pillows. A TV rests on a shelf hung from the ceiling at the foot of the bed. On one side of the head of the bed is a record player-cassette-radio console; in the far corners of the room, hidden by and rising from the jungles, are the speakers.

Bo designed the whole bedroom, but the speakers are creations. The technique is standard do-it-yourself plaster over chicken wire and wood frame, the inspiration pure Diddley. The plaster is slapped on in massive gobs and roughly molded by powerful hands. The speakers are about three feet high and the same width, and shaped like crumpled sea anemones, or the suction pads of octopi, or something else oozily subaqueous. Spray-painted black and gold, they are arresting sculpture, startlingly sexual and strange. Bo likes them. "Whatever I'm doing, I do my thing."

In the storeroom behind the studio there are a few more

speakers, but those are lost behind boxes of old tapes, appliances and toys: one box contains turbans Bo made his band wear a long time ago, some are filled with plain junk. "You ask, you just ask daddy what his favorite hobby is," Tan had said before, laughing, "and there's only one thing he can say truly, and that's digging in the dump. After music he likes dirt best." A true junkster, Bo didn't bother to defend himself, just reached into a cabinet and pulled out a beautiful antique cast-iron pot he had found. One recent find was a third-grader's spelling test from the 1930s—Bo dug it.

There are scrapbooks, too, ill-kept but bulging. Pictures of Bo smiling with djs at nightclub tables; pictures of his name on the Apollo marquee; on stage with Jerome and the Duchess (his younger half-sister, Norma Jean); beside an airport limousine which he once owned and painted up weird. One picture included the amp he built for himself in the 1950s: "I was the first cat I know to make amps bigger than what the companies would give you." There was a picture he had taken of himself a couple of years ago. In it he is standing beside a burnt-out stove and other trash; he is in raggedy overalls, no shirt, and his guitar is at his feet. A pitchfork is in one hand, the other is outstretched. "Took that on the ashes of my mother's house in McComb a few years back. The title is: 'Where do we go from here?'"

There were pictures, too, of other stars: Arthur Prysock, the Moonglows, Clyde McPhatter. "I got a few of Jackie Wilson," said Bo, leafing through the stacks; "he was a favorite of mine —he sure had a thing with those girls. And here are the Shirelles —now, they were beautiful, and nice to work with. Just did a job with them in Boston, one of those revival shows, and they're still great. Man, it's funny, here I am with all these stars, and now look at me. I been there with all the greatest, and I can't see why I didn't get further than I did."

From "Bo Diddley" in 1955 to the LP *Bo Diddley's a Gunslinger* in 1962, Bo was a star. He and Chuck Berry were Chess

Records' gold-dust twins, though Bo was never as big as Chuck. Chuck was a more clever hit maker than Bo, his lyrics snappier and his touch a trifle more pop-oriented. Bo's audience was smaller but perhaps more fanatical: once you had connected with Bo, it was hard to get loose. At the time some talked of a feud, but Bo says it's nonsense. "I never had no envious feelings toward Chuck. I never got too close to him. He was quiet back then just like he is now. I admit he's a strange dude, but I can get along with anybody."

Once established, Bo started working at the rock 'n' roll business, hard work indeed. It had a lot more flash and a little more money than blues club jobs, but it also included endless traveling and the psychological strain of having to "stay on top." Like Berry and dozens of others, Bo toured, wrote, and recorded for seven straight years. There was no time for vacations and no premium for development; you were only as good as your latest hit. It was not a way to get rich; on this point Bo is adamant.

"After my first record I started getting two hundred fifty dollars a gig, and I never got much more than that, even when I had the hottest record in the country. I had a band to pay, a car to run, and I was trying to send about a hundred bucks a week back to my family. Managers, hah! I used to wouldn't ask questions, because I figured the manager cat was in my corner, he was gonna do everything in his power to do my thing for me. No way!

"A guy would tell me, 'I got you covered, you play your axe, man, I'll do the rest.' So I say, 'Crazy,' and there I am, going down the road, two, three, four in the morning, sleeping on the road, doing my thing at gigs every night. Then I look for my money, and the man say, 'Oh, everything's all right, man.' And I say, 'Sure, it's fine for you, at home every night with your wife and kids, but when I get home I'm broke again.'

"I'm not gonna tell no lie and say, 'Yeah, because I'm Bo Diddley I got a whole lot of money.' I ain't got a quarter—by that I mean I ain't got the couple of hundred thousand in the bank I should have. Right now I'm not really in debt, but I wouldn't say I was out of debt either. I'm putting food on the table, and that's all. I have been robbed of what was really mine because I worked for it. I have been robbed of styles and arrangements, sounds, and I don't know who is getting the money, but I ain't. They told me once you can't copyright a beat. Hah!

"It was hard, man, it was hard. I wouldn't have the problems I have today if the record company had taken care of business and given me what was due. The record companies have got ways of getting around you, of b.s.-ing you. They say, 'Oh, man, you ain't sold but nine thousand records,' but they want to sign you again. Now why do they keep signing me if I ain't making them no business? Would you go out and pick up rotten apples if you can't sell 'em? But I took it. What else could I do? You danced to the tune they was playing, or you didn't dance at all."

Yet a few sentences later Bo could talk of Leonard and Phil Chess as "beautiful cats." By all accounts Chess Records was run like many ghetto businesses: the brothers (Phil is still alive; Leonard died in October, 1969) were tyrants, but their own tough Jewish souls kept them close to the artists whom, on some level, they truly loved. What other white man but Leonard Chess could call Sonny Boy Williamson "motherfucker" and get away with it? Chess' tape vaults will some day be recognized as a national treasure.

Bo has made over a dozen LPs for Chess, ranging from classics like *Bo Diddley Is a Lover* and *Have Guitar, Will Travel* to topically titled jobs like *Bo Diddley's a Twister, Surfin' with Bo Diddley,* and even *Bo Diddley's Beach Party.* As with all such albums, there is some repetition—*Roadrunner,* for instance, is a mixture of old and new material. But that was not Bo's doing, and in all the hours of music he made there is not one dull minute. *Bo Diddley's 16 All-Time Greatest Hits,* forty-five minutes of stunning rock 'n' roll music, is probably the best introduction to his music, but why stop there? He has written some of the most beautiful ballads in rock (like "Come On, Baby" on *Gunslinger* and "Love Is a Secret" on *Bo Diddley Is a Lover*), some guitar instrumentals (like "Spanish Guitar" on *Have Guitar*) that sound almost Arabic, and his tune "Mr. Khrushchev" stops the show on the *Bo Diddley* album, one of his best. His introduction to "Congo" on the *Lover* LP sounds like Jimi Hendrix ten years early.

Bo's musical gestures are so bold on record that one feels it was not so much that the microphones overheard his music, but that, like an artist working in plastic, Bo personally stamped his image on the vinyl discs. Every track is inimitably Bo's, not because they all sound the same—they vary widely in style—but because Bo's artistic vision is founded on a belief in his own uniqueness. "A person is an individual, and being an individual person is a gas," he said. "I have my own way of expressing my soulful feelings. I never wanted to be like anybody else, and I can't copy anybody else. I got my own bag of tricks."

All Bo's songs express that radical humanism. Sometimes called "the Originator," he finds his creative energy not in his environment or other musicians but within himself. That crude energy, coming from levels too mysterious for self-conscious control, vitalizes everything he makes. His power is shaman power, and like the devil he gives himself many names: the Puffessor, Doctor Diddley, Diddley Daddy, the Man Who Knows Everything, and, of course, Bo Diddley. Roadrunner and gunslinger too, he can take on any guise because he knows who he is.

His exulting in himself is both comic and cosmic. In "Hey, Bo Diddley," he's like Old McDonald with "women here, women there, women, women everywhere"; in "Gunslinger" he's got "a gun on his hip and a rose on his chest." In "Who Do You Love," one of his masterpeices (he also helped write "Love Is Strange"), he lets it all out:

> I got forty-seven miles of barbwire,
> I use a cobra snake as a necktie,
> I got a brand new house on the roadside,
> Made of rattlesnake hide,

*I got a brand new chimney made on top,*
*Made out of human skulls,*
*Now, c'mon, take a little walk with me, Arlene,*
*An' tell me, who do you love. . . .*
*Got a tombstone hand and a graveyard mind,*
*Just twenty-two and I don't mind dying,*
*Who do you love,*
*Yeah,*
*Who do you love?**

If his preening were vanity, he would not be sexy; as it is, Bo is one of the sexiest men in music. He loves women as much as he loves himself, and establishes his manhood only to prove the power of his feelings. "She's Alright" has almost no structure as a song; it's just Bo shouting about his "Mary Lou." "Dearest Darling" is a crooner's song with lyrics to match:

*I once had a heart so good and true,*
*But now it's gone from me to you,*
*Take care of it as I have done,*
*For you have two hearts and I have none.†*

Bo sings with unaffected simplicity and adds many grunts, moans and mammalian pleasure noises, so there's no mistaking what he's talking about. "I'm Sorry" is a perfect rock 'n' roll ballad with that stately pace that groups like the Penguins and the Moonglows were so good at, and Bo's ordered expression of his inchoate emotions fills the song with passion.

All his work is filled with good humor. "Say, Man," which is Bo and Jerome trading insults ("You're so ugly your mother had to put a sheet over your head so sleep could slip up on you"),

*"Who Do You Love" By Ellas McDaniel
©1958 Arc Music Corp. Used with permission of the publisher; all rights reserved.
†"Dearest Darling" by Ellas McDaniel
© 1958 Arc Music Corp. Used with permission of the publisher; all rights reserved.

is all jokes and ends with a joke on itself: an unidentified third party (in fact Bo) sticks his head in and agrees with either one or both. When Bo says in "Roadrunner," "Gonna put some dirt in your eye!" and then laughs, you know he means it. The humor is not just the jokes; it is Bo's whole stance. He obviously enjoys making records, and that enjoyment comes through in the music. Bo feels free to talk directly to the listener: in Willie Dixon's "You Can't Judge a Book by the Cover," he commands, "You got your radio turned down too low. Turn it up!"

Bo's music is, however, more in his rhythm than in his words or melodies; most of the latter are skeletal or non-existent. The phrase, "the Bo Diddley beat," suggests a formula; rather, that his beat has been named is a tribute to him, one of the great rhythm makers in rock 'n' roll. Bo can play fine solo blues guitar, but mostly he plays rhythm. Playing on the neck, below the pick-ups, along the strings, and even tapping the body, he gets an astonishing dynamic range to his beats. He can make his guitar talk, creating phrases with sentencelike inflections; sometimes he sounds a bit like Donald Duck. In concert he often does long solos, building rhythms and cross-rhythms into hypnotically fascinating structures. He starts almost every song himself; their drive is always his. I cannot describe Bo Diddley's many beats in words besides saying that they are infectious, joyous, and strong as the man himself.

Bo called it his "thing" and doesn't underestimate its importance in communicating his art. "It's my rhythm that makes my music penetrate to the followers I have. What you do has got to penetrate. You can be a good speaker and know what to say, but if you ain't shooting it out right, it just ain't gonna do right. You almost gotta write it on a piece of paper and sing it at the same time, just so as to make sure people don't misunderstand. You got to get it out there, *produce* it, make the people feel it, and if they like it, well, you got something going."

If Bo's peak was in 1962, his fall came swiftly on its heels. One effect of the Beatles' arrival on the scene was to make the idols of the 1950s memories instead of stars. Bo was a hit in England

—where he became close friends with the Rolling Stones—but in America the kids wanted the English boys who idolized and imitated Bo. With every year Bo's old fans grew further from their record-buying teenage years. Bo, no longer riding the crest, had to check his finances more closely. That inevitably led to run-ins at Chess.

"The minute I started speaking up, right away the cats are saying, 'Well, it looks like this black boy is getting smart.' Man, do you know I've never gotten a check in the mail from Chess Records? Royalties?—a joke. Ever since I been there it seems like *I* owe *Chess.*" He rummaged through a stack of old mail and found a letter from Chess (now part of the GRT Corporation) he had received a few months before. It was a bill for studio time, instrument rental, hotel rooms and other miscellaneous charges; it added up to thirty-nine thousand dollars. "Are you ready for that?" asked Bo. He threw the paper down.

"I got rid of my last Cadillac years ago; I let it go back to the collection people. Chess, they wanted me to have it. What for? My car don't play nothing. A cat with a big car is showing off his equipment; the cat who pulls up with a raggedy car and his instruments falling out—watch him, he's dangerous. I decided I wasn't falling for that flashy trick bag no more. When I stopped taking those new Cadillacs, the Chess brothers they got worried. They knew they had nothing to bribe me with no more."

By the mid-1960s his relations with Chess were so bad that Bo made the crucial decision: to stop recording, stop hoping that one more record would break the cycle. He moved his family to California from Chicago, beginning the exile in which he is still living. Two years ago, when I first thought of interviewing Bo, Chess representatives discouraged me, saying Bo was a "difficult cat" who had inexplicably hidden himself away. To Chess, Bo's decision probably was inexplicable: who ever heard of a black artist rejecting Cadillacs and going on strike?

Idleness has been hard on Bo. For weeks at a time he does not know when his next gig will be. He makes calls to get work but has to watch that he doesn't wear out his welcome where one is extended. He's done time stewing in his own juices, and though he has nothing to do with politics, he has a mordant view of the American Way. Americans, he says, "are great believers in b.s. They love to listen to it; the truth—they don't want to hear." He's never liked cops—"I've been shoved up against the wall a few times, in jail for stuff I didn't know about, and that created a little dislike"—and he has little respect for the Establishment in general. "Those judges and lawyers and people who have already had their day, they is sitting on top of their money, they is got the keys, and is keeping the top *securely* fastened. They have everything they want, and if they ain't got it, they's probably stealing it through some way a bookkeeper is doing for them. I know the whole scene. Look how it works for us musicians: everybody likes our records, even the people who owns the banks, but nobody wants to give us credit. We is well loved, but we is bad risks. Hah!"

Fortunately, the bitterness is balanced by deep religious faith. The Bible is *the* book for Bo, and as he gets his beat from the sanctified church, he draws his world-view from his Baptist upbringing. "Some things in the Bible I don't understand. I shake my head and say, 'Maybe I'll come across somebody with better answers one day, but until then I'll let it be.' " One thing he does know is that he is a man because he is a son of Adam. "We are all sons and daughters of him and Eve—the Bible don't mention anybody else getting it all started—so we are all sisters and brothers. Man has got to get it together for himself. Do you know we are the only animal that kills for the hell of it? We preach love and practice hate; we preach peace and practice war. Harmony, man, people getting along with themselves and each other, it would be so beautiful."

Those sentiments put him foursquare behind "the kids": "The white kids started digging what we were laying down because finally it was time for a change. They got tired of listening to Tchaikovsky and all them cats that their mommies and daddies were throwing at them. Tired of always playing the music real *low* so you could carry on a conversation while the music is in the background. The kids decided they wanted to use the record players for all the power they had. Pops and moms still don't understand what's happening."

From exile he watched the spread of rock 'n' roll after the Beatles, the success of his friends the Rolling Stones, the growth of the longhair culture, and he dug it. "When the Beatles came out with that 'Yeah, yeah, yeah' stuff, 'It's been a hard day's night,' " he sang with a big smile, "the old folks said, 'How cute.' Then a few weeks later they look around, and there's Junior, and they say, 'Junior, when you gonna get a haircut?' And pretty soon Junior's hair is down to *here!* Hah! *Man, if I could grow my hair long, I'd grow it down to the ground!*

"All this talk about a generation gap? It's the parents who created it. The kids are trying to tell 'em what's happening in words, music, dress and all, but the parents won't understand. They slam the door; they is belligerent. I've seen it happen at these festivals; the cops call it a riot, but it's the cops who start it. They call one off saying there is *gonna* be a riot—how can they know that unless it's them who makes 'em?"

Bo knows he has a place in this musical and social movement, but he hasn't known how to get it. He wears home tie-dyed jeans on stage now, and would like to organize with other musicians to do low-cost cooperative gigs—"We could play schoolyards Saturday afternoons and make it a buck a head or something." The recent much-publicized "rock 'n' roll revival" got his name around, but it put him in an "oldie but goldie" bag he doesn't like. To combat that, he went back to Chess studios in 1970 and made *Black Gladiator*. Phil Chess was the producer —Bo would deal with no one else. The LP was released at the same time as Chuck Berry's *Home Again*, his first record on Chess for six years, and together they got the old-home-week treatment.

*Black Gladiator* is a totally fresh record, bursting, exploding, and just plain rocking with Bo's energy. The title and theme are in a direct line with "I'm a Man." as Bo explains it, "Man is supposed to be built. Look at the gladiators back in Roman days. These cats could walk up and hit a mule, deck a horse by cracking him on the jaw. Man is getting out of that; try it today and you break your hand. We are living too fast. We are using the knowledge box more, doing less of a physical thing. Like my wife says, and she makes sense, 'We're gonna be all head and no body after a while.' I believe it should be more balanced than that." Or, as he sings, "Don't write a check with your mouth you can't cash with your tail.'"

The record starts with "Elephant Man"; two other songs are "Power House" and "You, Bo Diddley" (as in, "Who's the greatest man in town? You, Bo Diddley"). Everything sounds the way the back jacket photo looks: Bo, guitar in hand, his head back, singing, his mouth wide open, his bare chest and arms in studded leather belts—he designed the suit himself and had it made by a tailor in Montreal.

Side two opens with "I've Got a Feeling," and that feeling is that Bo's "gonna be happy for once in [his] life." The old "Hush Your Mouth" has become "Shut Up, Woman," in which Bo gives his woman an epic talking-to, but only because he knows that "I'm yours, and you'se mine. . . . We *love* one another." "I Don't Like You" is funnier than the original "Say, Man." "If you don't watch out, you is gonna play mountain and get climbed on," warns Bo's antagonist. *"Start climbing, baby,"* Bo grunts back. It also introduces Bo the opera singer, a side of himself he had concealed until now. "But I've always had that voice. In Sunday-school choir, even when I was in the back row, when I got to *singing,* the teacher would stop everything and tell me to hush up."

*Black Gladiator* is Bo Diddley at his very best, not a revived memory but an artist at the height of his powers. A subsequent record, *Pollution,* is less successful; a new producer gave him current rock hits to cover. Bo does his best, but he's in unfamiliar waters. When he sings a line by Al Kooper—"I could have been the president of General Motors"—his disbelief is comically obvious. Maybe Al Kooper could have been, but Bo knows better than that. Chess Records, now part of a New York-based conglomerate, is not the Chess of old, and Bo's recording future is still uncertain.

In person, however, Bo is better than ever, in full command of the stage and audience from the moment he steps to the mike: "The only person I ever feared on stage is Ray Charles." He has hopes that his days in exile are close to over; he'd much rather be making music than fixing cars. At a recent concert in San Francisco's Civic Auditorium he lifted both arms above his head, signaling for silence. It came immediately. "Forty-three years ago tonight, a wonderful thing happened in the world," he announced, then paused dramatically. "I was born." Cheers from the crowd. Again his hands up, again silence. "In honor of that occasion, I have a new song to sing." It was a slow ballad with the recurrent line, "I love you, I love you, I love you." When done, he looked out at the audience, a hand shading his eyes against the spotlights. "Hey, everybody," he said, "I'm Doctor Diddley, the Puffessor—what you got on your mind?— I got the answer." There was a ripple of laughter.

"Have mercy. But there's one thing I want you to know, one thing you gotta dig with Bo: I *understand.*" Silence greeted that; maybe Bo's eyes were burning too brightly. He pulled back a bit.

"And I remember, too, that without you who are so beautiful I wouldn't have made it at all with what you might call the rock 'n' roll music. Thank you, thank you, thank you, from the bottom of my heart. You see, I'm always *your* Bo Diddley."

The hall responded with a murmur and scattered clapping. Bo smiled, hit a chord, and called the next tune to the band. He looked back at the audience. "I thank you in advance for the great round of applause I am about to get."

● Ralph Bass is a hipster. He's got a droopy red mustache and tousled red hair, wears shades and jump suits, and talks more spade than Lord Buckley. Remember those smoke-throated late-night jazz djs, coming on so cool in the fifties, playing Count Basie and Ellington and flipping over sassy Sarah Vaughan and Billy Eckstine? Bass is of their school, one of those white men who fell so in love with black music and musicians that they not

RALPH BASS

only collected records and hung around the bars and after hours clubs, but took a hand in making the music and eventually became part of the black show-biz world that produced it.

Bass is (now for Chess) a producer; he started with live jazz shows in the forties around LA and then moved inevitably into rhythm-and-blues. His first big record was "Open the Door, Richard" by Jackie McVea, a novelty number turned out in the last four minutes of a four-hour record session. Back in those days he was cutting directly onto sixteen-inch lacquer master discs—everything on one track and no mistakes allowed. He worked for several companies—some were his own—in the tangled world of "off-brand" records. Many of the tiny labels were founded by juke-box owners who, with wartime rationing, had to go into production to ensure themselves full boxes.

Today the rock 'n' roll–rhythm-and-blues industry is a business apparently as lush and fashionable as the chic record covers or the velvet roll of a star's collar. A facade is a facade is a facade. A quick perusal of the "trades," *Billboard* or *Cashbox* magazines, indicates that making and selling plastic music is not much different from making and selling plastic anything. When Ralph Bass started there was no facade. Bass is not a jet-setting producer with complex "recording concepts," but a hustling cat who loves life and music and who does his best to get it all on wax. Lying comfortably on a hotel bed (on a break from recording Etta James), he drawled out his story, moving quickly over the days when he recorded Erroll Garner and Dexter Gordon, and going into detail on the early fifties when he started doing rhythm-and-blues. The following is an abridged version of the interview.

*Bass:* It was during this period [1950–51] that I found a group called the Dominoes which was featuring a cat named Clyde McPhatter. Billy Ward was their vocal coach. The cat came into my office, I was in New York then with Federal, my own label for King Records, and the cat had a dub of an aircheck from some radio talent show and wanted me to hear it. The group was doing a thing like "Goodnight, Irene" or something. I said,

"Man, I can't use this." He says, "Man, it won the contest." I says, "Man, the thing hasn't got it." But he was so insistent, I said bring the group down. So they came in, and Billy Ward said, "What's wrong with the group?" I said, "This ain't fish nor fowl, it ain't pop enough to be pop, it ain't R&B enough to be R&B. It's in between, it ain't got a 'thing.' " So he said, "What kind of music you want to hear?" So I started playing records for him. There was an old group called the Orioles, it was the only group out at the time that was selling. And Ward, said, "I can write songs like that all the time," so I says, "Baby, write me *one.*" When I heard his song, I was real enthused. We went into the studio in New York and did a thing called "Do Something for Me" with Clyde McPhatter. I got on the phone, called the old man Syd Nathan, and says, "Man, we got something." Sure enough it was a hit. The rest is history; the Dominoes became a top group.

Then Jackie Wilson joined the group. They fired Clyde McPhatter, because he didn't dig Billy Ward. Ward was a slave driver, and Clyde couldn't make no money; he was on salary, the group was on salary. Clyde got some offers from other companies, Atlantic was one of them, and Clyde made the change, and Billy fired him 'cause he had rules and regulations—like they were supposed to be in at a certain time, and they couldn't talk to girls and shit like that while they were working. So then Jackie came in. The next group I found were a group called the Midnighters with Hank Ballard. Hank wasn't with the group when I first recorded them. I did a thing with another lead singer, and it had the nucleus of a sound, and Hank Ballard joined the group, and we did things like "Work with Me, Annie," "Sexy Ways," just one thing after another—"Annie Had a Baby."

*ML:* What about censorship in those days?

*Bass:* Censorship at that time was very tough. All the people who were on the radio stations were tough because they valued their licenses. If you had a black station you figured you gotta be twice as cool as the other cats, so they were screening every-thing. Hank's tunes, they were scared to death of them.

You see, we were making records for R&B, weren't thinking in terms of white kids, but it so happened that at this particular time white kids were starting to listen to R&B shows and they were bringing these records home. If you don't understand the language, the connotation is dirty, baby; we whites got our ways of talking about sex, blacks have their way, and see, with the white it would be cute whereas with the black it got to be dirty. That was the thing, that was the concept. With "Work with Me, Annie," they had a big thing in Los Angeles about the dirty lyrics, and they were taking my song as the thing. There was a TV talk show, and they were going to talk about dirty records, and I said I would like to be there to defend myself, because they had a cat from the PTA, and they had a little thirteen-year-old girl, they had this politician, and they had a priest or a minister on the show. So I got on the show, and I said, "You take 'Work with Me, Annie': there's no implication in the word 'work.' It could mean anything, it was a jazz word. It's just an expression. I'm gonna tell you about some more songs, some of the songs that whites know, like 'Making Whoopee.'" I said, "Hear what that man say? That's what you get for making whoopee—you get a baby. Now that's dirty, why don't you say that's dirty? Oh no, that's *cute*. Well, that's cute because our words is cute to you, 'making whoopee.' Yet 'Work with Me, Annie' is dirty because you don't know what 'work' means." I said, "You take these billboards. What does a woman half un-dressed, her breasts all hanging out, with a bottle of beer, what's that got to do with a bottle of beer? Well, that's cute, that's alright, isn't it. Take 'Hernando's Hideaway.' What are they hiding in Hernando's Hideaway? But that's cute."

Next group I had was the Five Royals, great gospel group, and then the Platters. I heard a guy named Tony Williams at a club, thought he was great and put him with a group called the Platters, but they weren't really together. So a cat come to my office and said he'd like to record the Platters. I said, "Who are you?" and he said, "Buck Ram." He asked if I was going to record them, and I said I thought they were great, and he said he'd coach them, and we made a deal. But we lost them because Buck wanted some money for them doing some background vocal. And Syd said, "Well, they're only worth fifty dollars. I can get anyone I want to do 'doo wahs' and "oodle oohs." " So Buck said, "For fifty bucks? If you think that much of my group, then give me a release." And Syd did. And I had done "Only You." It was in the can. They had come in two hours late for a session, man, and we did one take of "Only You," and the first thing they did for Mercury was "Only You," and that was the thing that kicked them off. And then came James Brown. James Brown was probably—oh, everybody knows James Brown. Getting him was like a James Bond story; I found him down in Georgia.

*ML:* You discovered James Brown?

*Bass:* I heard a dub, and it was so different that it knocked me out, cleaned me. I said, "Where can I find him?" I was in Atlanta, Georgia, at the time. It wasn't called James Brown, it was a group named the Famous Flames. So a disc jockey and I drove to Macon, Georgia, from Atlanta in a pouring rainstorm, pouring like crazy, and I found out that James had a manager named Clint Brandly who had a nightclub and was the local promoter. James was out on parole to Brandly at the time.

*ML:* What was he in for?

*Bass:* James had a very hard young life. James was a "society outcast." Since Macon was such a Jim Crow town, I was told to meet Brandly by parking my car in front of a barbershop which was right across the street from a railroad station, and when the venetian blinds went up and down, to come on in. And I did. And I looked at Brandly, and the cat said, "Yeah, I got a contract from Leonard Chess in my hand, I was waiting for Leonard Chess." Well, Leonard Chess *was* on his way, 'cause Leonard always said to me, "I'll never forgive you 'cause you beat me to James Brown." That was one thing Leonard always kept saying to me. Now, he was on his way, but see, in those days, man, airplanes, if the weather was halfway bad, they couldn't come in. They had no radar and all that jive they have today, and so he was grounded. Well anyway I gave the cat two hundred dollars and I said, "Do you want to sign right now?" He says, "You got a deal. Call the whole group in to sign the papers." I don't know James Brown from a hole in the ground, and I went to the club that night and saw him do his show, crawling on his stomach and saying "please, please, please—" he must have said please for about ten minutes.

*ML:* He was the only cat who had ever done that crazy stuff?

*Bass:* Well, no, that was an old thing. Big Jay McNeely, he used to do a thing with the saxophone, crawl with his body. It was a common thing, Wolf did it. James had seen it someplace. I almost got fired for doing the record. After I collected my two hundred dollars that I paid out and paid for the expenses, I went back to St. Louis, and they sent some people looking for me to tell me I was fired. I called the old man up and asked Syd what's wrong. He says, "Man, you cut the worst piece of shit I ever heard in my life." I said, "What you talking about?" He says, "Man, this man sounds like he's stoned on the record, all he's saying is one word." I said, "Oh, you mean 'please.'" He says, "Yeah, all he's saying is 'please, please, please, please, please.'" I says, "Well, I'll tell you what, put the record out in Atlanta, Georgia, and if it don't sell, baby, don't fire me, I quit. I'll walk clear all over the country to show you how bad this record is." Well, the rest is history. Who knew then that James would be what he is today?

*ML:* Was he just a country kid then?

*Bass:* Yes he was, he used to call me Mister Ralph. He was so browbeaten with that shit down there. I says, "Well man, don't call me no Mister Ralph. Either call me Mister Bass or call me Ralph, but don't call me no Mister Ralph."

*ML:* How did you get along with the black guys in the business then?

*Bass:* I guess I got along with them 'cause nothing ever happened to me. I was straight and cool and able to get my gigs. I got along beautifully. You had to feel your way, well it had to be kind of a natural thing.

*ML:* Were there many white people doing it?

*Bass:* All of the independent companies, except for a few, were all white. They had to do the same thing I was doing. And the spades expected the white cat to come in and do something. He was the man that had the bread, not only the bread but had the know-how, how to make records. 'Cause there was nothing down in the South, everything was up North, see. And the black kids didn't know where to go to do it. They didn't come to you, you went and found them. Now they're hip, they come to you.

*ML:* How did you go out and find them?

*Bass:* I had to go out there and look and beat the bushes.

*ML:* Did you go out to clubs every night?

*Bass:* Among other things, but it wasn't just a matter of going out to clubs, you'd get a tip on somebody, go down to listen to somebody. You know how it is: someone say, "Man, why don't you hear so-and-so," and you go down and listen. And I was fortunate in being able to recognize what was good and what was wrong. There's no such thing as a genius, baby. I mean, like if there was, the cat could make a billion dollars. But I found a lot of bodies. More than my share.

*ML:* Did you have a style?

*Bass:* No, just what I felt. All my things were unique and different, that was the saying. I think you got a chance if you're unique and different. You may not sell, but you got a chance.

*ML:* Were you doing instrumentals and vocals all at one time?

*Bass:* Oh, yes, there was no overdubbing. One-track mono, and no remixing, we'd balance it up right there. Then we went to a two-track thing, the vocal on one, whole band on the other, so we could dub if we had to.

*ML:* The white people who were making this music were way ahead of their time in their involvement in black culture, not just cocktail parties with NAACP doctors like most whites of the fifties.

*Bass:* We were in the ghetto. There were no rich black kids who were singing. There were a few who came out from good families, like Miles Davis, his father was a doctor. Mostly the kids were from the ghettos, from broken homes.

*ML:* How did you happen to dig it all, and how did your own family dig it?

*Bass:* I did this as a personal sacrifice. My first wife couldn't understand it, my parents couldn't understand it, they didn't know what I was doing. In fact, none of my white friends knew, they didn't know what rhythm-and-blues was. They said to me one day, "What kind of music do you make," 'cause I couldn't ever discuss it with them. What am I gonna discuss with them, you know? So I say, "Rhythm-and-blues." "What is that?" I say, "Well, I can't describe it to you, I'm gonna play some of it for you." They got real excited, you know, said "Ooh, where can you buy records like that?" Well, I knew it was just a matter of time. I went through all kinds of changes to get my thing done.

*ML:* Would you say before you'd gotten into this that you had been a regular white American?

*Bass:* I didn't know anything about black people 'cause I came from the ghetto in New York. We had Irish kids and German kids and Jewish kids in one block, and we used to fight like hell. We fought amongst ourselves, it was an ethnic thing, but it wasn't a racial thing. The first black kid I think I ever met was when I went to Stuyvesant High School in New York. 125th Street was ten miles away. Like in the twenties, you know, when you went a hundred miles up in the Catskills, it was a twenty-four hour ordeal. 125th Street was like eighty-nine miles away. Then later on I was exposed to black music 'cause I was playing some society bands, playing violin, and we'd stop up in Harlem during Prohibition and get some bathtub gin, and then we'd go hear Duke playing the Cotton Club, one of those places, Small's Paradise, all the black joints. The whites used to go up there and slum, they'd call it slumming, going up to Harlem. Being a musician, the music just fascinated me, 'cause it was quite a contrast playing society music and listening to this thing. I was fascinated. I would just sit there and watch the bodies sway. It was sensuous to me, the music itself, very emotional. It was an earthy kind of thing, this is what grabbed me. And that was my early beginning of digging this kind of music.

*ML:* What were you doing during the thirties?

*Bass:* I was working, shit I don't know, everything, I was working on Wall Street, working for a brokerage house. I was serving bottled water in California. I did everything—I drove a truck, I was a barker in front of a theater in Hollywood. I did everything, who could pick their job, man? To be a gasoline service attendant you had to be a college grad, you know. Rough times, you just did what you could find, and that's when I found myself.

I couldn't find myself until I went into music. I would take jobs and quit jobs, only because I didn't dig what I was doing.

*ML:* When did you go to Chess?

*Bass:* About 1960. I produced James for about a year and a half, then I quit King and went with Leonard. I brought Etta James to Chess, Moms Mabley, and Pigmeat Markham too. The Chess thing gave me a chance to work with some of the great blues artists—Muddy, Sonny Boy, and Wolf—and also to work with Ramsey Lewis. I had never worked with a name act before, all the acts I had ever worked with were acts that I discovered myself. I had to know them from the beginning, there had to be a rapport between me and the act, a thing of respect. You see, it's different when you discover somebody 'cause they feel within themselves that you had some part in their success by being there. And it's different with a big top name, you got to start communicating again. And psychologically, you have to be able to communicate with them, you have to understand your act, know where the weakness is and the strength—this is part of being an A&R man. Every producer got a different thing, whatever works for him that's fine. Generally speaking, I would say that you got to have some rapport with your act and respect both ways, dig and understand them, and to know what type of material they need and how to satisfy their egos, because great talent is messed up, you know, great talented ego. A cat that's a great artist, a great act, man, he's entitled to be egotistical, I mean he's entitled to his little thing. But don't let acts that ain't got nothing on the ball take the same attitude.

*ML:* You used to go out on the road with your acts. Why?

*Bass:* I wanted to *find out;* look, here's a grey cat who's making music for blacks, but he doesn't have no real knowledge of the deep South, not even as a white man. The white man down there only see what he want to see, and he wasn't allowed to really get into the black areas and go to the black clubs 'cause he was off limits; there were ordinances against the mixing of the races in public. So I wanted to see what it was like and where the music came from; why, how it came, dig? I went, and I realized on these one-nighters that people from a hundred miles would come around and see us, 'cause we were a big act. Little Esther and Johnny Otis. And like they would come from all over. And then I would sit there and realize, "What else did they have?" They couldn't go to a movie 'cause they had no black movies; maybe in the big, big cities they did, but not in the small towns. They couldn't go to any public place, you know, what did they have left? They had little clubs, and when an act came in, boom, that was it. Then I realized here they were, they were drinking, having a ball, escaping, escaping all of the taboos, all the shit they had to live with down in the South, so this was their way, this was one night when they could sing what they liked, when they thought that life was beautiful. And the great thing for me was to realize that I was giving them something to escape to even for a second, you know, and then I really started feeling it. Before it was what I could see in the big cities, but down in the South well, let's face it, it was still slavery, no matter what you called it, it was still slavery. They still had a thing going on with blacks, an economic thing, a stranglehold on them for cheap labor. Like it was a revelation to me, the whole tour. The first time. Then, of course, I spent most of my time in the deep South, looking for talent.

*ML:* How did you travel with the black acts? Different cars or something?

*Bass:* Same car, baby, and I stayed in the same hotel whenever I could. Sneak me in, sneak me out. I wanted to be with the cats, man, you know. I wanted to see where they was. I'm trying to get instant understanding, you know. But like I was the one who stayed in the kitchens and they used to eat in the dining room, 'cause we'd be going to the soul places in private homes, and

I'd be in the kitchen eating because I wasn't supposed to be there. But I dug soul food too.

*ML:* When did it start to break, when did the white kids start coming into the clubs?

*Bass:* In many areas the blacks would let the kids come in, they had a thing with the promoter—in these towns the promoter was the connecting link between the white establishment and the black community. He was usually the richest man, he had property and the political thing that went on, so they gave him a little ball, let the whites come over once in a while. Then they got "white spectator tickets" for the worst corner of the joint, no chairs and no dancing. But they had to keep enlarging it anyway, 'cause they just couldn't keep the white kids out, and by the early fifties they'd have white nights, or they'd put a rope across the middle of the floor. The blacks on one side, whites on the other, digging how the blacks were dancing and copying them. Then, hell, the rope would come down, and they'd all be dancing together. And you know it was a revolution. Music did it. We did it as much with our music as the civil rights acts and all of the marches, for breaking the race thing down.

*ML:* Were you aware of that at the time?

*Bass:* Of course I was, I saw it. Well, white kids—this was music that was growing on them, and their parents couldn't tell them not to buy the records, and they certainly couldn't tell them what to listen to on the radio. We know this, we know that when the first civil rights act was passed in 1955, the politicians in the South instructed the radio stations not to play any records by blacks. Nat "King" Cole, he was okay, and all the popular black acts, that were singing popular music, but not rhythm-and-blues. And they told all the storekeepers not to display merchandise that had pictures of blacks on it. We had to repackage all of our Earl Bostick LPs. But despite that the kids said, "Look, you ain't gonna tell us what to listen to," and they started tuning out the stations that wouldn't play that kind of music, the music they dug.

*ML:* When did the business become profitable for you?

*Bass:* At first I was making sixty dollars a week, but when I had a publishing company, Armo at King, and a percentage production deal—which was unheard of—then I made money. I published all the Hank Ballard stuff, I even have "Kansas City" by Leiber and Stoller. They were just two kids in New York, and I wanted to sign them as exclusive writers, but Syd Nathan said, "They'll never write another friggin' line." Good kids: Mike was serious cat, Lee a real hotshot.

*ML:* Are you a rich man now?

*Bass:* No, unfortunately my things were done in an era where . . . See, a producer today, he has a couple of hits, baby, boom! he wants seven percent, and because there are so many record companies who would bid for his services, he becomes hot with a couple of things. In my time where could you go? The majors weren't interested in R&B.

*ML:* What was Leonard Chess like?

*Bass:* One of the greatest men I ever knew. The cat had a feeling for little people that was so beautiful. He had an understanding about human nature; no education, but he could quote parables to make a point. He had a grasp of how people worked, and had a way of having people loyal to him. He would come right to the point. When you spoke to Leonard, man, you had to get there, say your thing, and you better do it within the first thirty seconds, and get the hell out.

*ML:* How did Atlantic fit in with the other independents?

*Bass:* Well, they had a cat who came up the same time I did, Herb Abramson, he founded it, it was his brains. The Erteguns, they were kind of rich sons from a diplomatic family or something. They came from a very fine family, a moneyed family, and they were doing it for kicks. They didn't have to do it for a living really. They gravitated to it, then Jerry Wexler came into the picture. There's a whole thing about Atlantic Records which I don't even want to discuss. It would be just too much hearsay without any definite proof of how the company really started and who really owned it. But they eased Herb out. It was a personal thing, a domestic thing with his wife and the partners. He went to the Korean War, came back, and they bought him out. But he was the guiding light, the brains, not the business thing so much as the creative thing. Jerry was just a businessman, but like, you know, he knew how to put the bodies together, that was the important thing in this business.

Today's conception of a producer is that he has to be a writer, an arranger or leader. But I think the greatest cat to be a producer is someone who doesn't even know music, because he has no musical prejudices for one thing, and just as long as he has an ear and knows what's commercial and knows how to put bodies together, things together, that's actually what "producer" means, the right combination. And he's not hung up with prejudices like being a musician or an arranger. But today they figure a producer can write, he's a songwriter, or an arranger or a musician.

*ML:* How much did black guys talk about race prejudice back in the fifties?

*Bass:* No, baby, we didn't talk much about race prejudice, 'cause there was nobody to inflame us, there was no movement as such. It was the way it was, and we judged a cat by his ability, black or white. If he was a great musician, well, what difference? There was no thing about black and white within our confines. What went on within their minds when they went to bed, I can't say. All I can say is how it was when we were together face to face. Of course there must have been so many blocks in their minds—I mean, really messed up. It had to be, but we were in show business, you know? Respect, there was respect anyway.

There's a thing going on now that I really don't dig, like, with R&B—hire nothing but black—of course the black-white ratio has been off balance in executive jobs. We don't want to perpetuate the other thing in reverse, it would be the same thing. However, it's a very delicate thing. And like, man, I paid my dues, I ain't got anything to prove anymore. I can't take it seriously unless anybody offends me. Even him I look at, and I have to crack up. He don't know who I am, he thinks I'm some square? And you know, it's a sensitive thing, but I've been to shows and I've been to conventions, and these cats can be aroused in seconds now. Somebody up there say, "Hey, we got the bird?" They think emotionally rather than try to think rationally. That's the time when communication lines break down.

*ML:* Did you really love producing?

*Bass:* Oh man, it was my whole life. I sacrificed my family for it. I think this is the only way you can do anything, either you go in or you stay out, no half measures. If you have the thing, this is you, and this is your projection, and this is your contribution to life. Damn the money; I didn't make that much money to start off with, but dig: I could live off nostalgia for years if I did nothing else. I feel I took part in an important part of history, musical history. And I felt that I accomplished something, I felt that I left the world something. You know, we all want to leave here doing something constructive in the world. Like, I contributed something, man.

*ML:* What do you think it is that you contributed?

*Bass:* I contributed a music and a togetherness in the form of music today. It had to be cats like myself who struggled, who believed in it, who made possible what happened later on. Not to say that if I wasn't there it wouldn't have happened, but it was through cats like myself. And we worked for it, because it was hard work, it wasn't easy.

*ML:* How did it happen that you went from the sophistication of forties jazz, Parker and Dizzy Gillespie, to believing in Hank Ballard?

*Bass:* Sometimes concepts change, like the truth is revealed to you, boom! Like I saw the light. One day I sat in Birdland, I forget who was playing, and the crowd was standing back to back, and everybody was shaking their heads, and I looked and thought, "I don't think there is one cat here who understands what he is playing." Then I realized the cat was playing for himself, he was completely out of it, into his own thing. I didn't understand what he was feeling. If you're entertaining, play for me, baby, let me understand what you're doing; you're trying to communicate with your heart. But this cat was playing something that knocked him out, not the public. It was selfish music, man, great but selfish. How many people dig all those chord changes, the patterns? Not the public. I'm trying to say that music is a definite emotion. Don't force anything on me, let me feel it, whatever it might be. And don't ridicule me for my likes in music, 'cause I won't stand for it, baby. If it kills me or kills you, it has served its purpose. What difference does it make whether it's acid rock, country, folk, classical, opera—if it does something for you, that's the important thing. I don't particularly care for the Beatles as a great singing act, but, man, they're talented, they rate, their conception really kills me, dig? And that's important; if we would only relate that to other things than music, it would be a beautiful world.

*ML:* How do you like modern soul music?

*Bass:* First, I'd like to object to the word "soul." If you call soul the influence of the black Baptist church, the implication is that that's the only kind of soul. But a Jewish cat got his kind of soul, an Italian cat his, and so on. I always liked black "soul." It was the funk of it. You must remember there's a similarity about being raised a Jew and black. When the cantor would sing the chants in synagogue in minor keys, it was like the bluesman singing in minor keys, so the blues was a familiar sound in my ears. Most people don't dig minor keys—they know it has a sad sound, the story it tells them they don't want to hear—but it was home to me.

Now I'm working on something I call "gos-pop." Gospel has so much to say, it's been the root of big soul, but gospel is slowly dying. We gotta get through the purism in gospel. The old gospel disc jockeys insist on playing the pure gospel thing, but young people don't want to hear about J.C. like they used to. They want a religion of "what am I doing in this world?" It's still religion, and I give it a beat that they can dance to.

*ML:* Like "Happy Day?"

*Bass:* Yeah, that's more pop, but that came out after I had got the idea of gos-pop down, and it just happened that somebody else got the hit on it first.

*ML:* Back to the South; were you ever arrested down there?

*Bass:* Yeah, I was arrested in Dallas. I was set up by a treasury man, he became a very dear friend of mine later on. He thought I was a pusher, man, thought the record business was a front. What's a white cat doing down there with blacks all the time? And that kind of music? In the fifties, man, how many whites knew what rhythm-and-blues was? So you know I had to be pretty careful in my life 'cause I knew I was under surveillance.

But I've never smoked a stick in my life, I've never had a benny, I've never had a pill. The reason I don't is 'cause I don't need it, I get in the mood naturally.

*ML:* What's the most complicated recording technique you work with now?

*Bass:* Four-track is my thing. Eight-track is when you're not sure of yourself, you've got everything on a separate track. Actually you lose excitement. Once I did a thing simultaneously. On one machine I did two-track, and on another machine it was mono, everything together. We could never get the excitement out of the two-track we could get out of the mono. I don't know what it is, can't explain it. Was it overtones? I don't know, but the blend wasn't natural. It wasn't *right there.* I'm old-fashioned. Stereo bothers me; the left ear gets adjusting to the left speaker and the right ear adjusting to the right one, and next thing my ears are hurting because my left ear is straining to the left side and my right is straining opposite. I don't dig the weird effects and jive, man, for myself. I just love to hear, well, it's the funk, man. How do you describe funk? I couldn't, it's a feeling. It's an emotional reaction, or a conclusion your ears come to. I just don't dig tricks, just don't dig panning back and forth, you know. I like pure listening, listening to the music for the sake of music itself.

● In the heart of Brooklyn start avenues which, with few bends or interruptions, run for miles into Long Island's flat expanse. The tenements of treeless neighborhoods give way in Jamaica to shaded row houses which by slow degrees become more suburban until, in Elmont, each house stands by itself with tailored front and back yards. The avenues change less than the neighborhoods through which they pass: they are devoted to

THE CHIFFONS

commerce of every type. Each brick building with its distinctive treatment of cornice and window details—no matter how shabby, nor whether it shelters rug outlet, wig shop, or bakery (dentist upstairs)—patiently serves the process of get and spend.

All day the traffic crawls, and the sidewalks are full of people waiting, walking, talking, eating custards from Carvel, and carrying home new lamps from Schwartz's and plastic wastebaskets from the discount hardware. Each block may be a unique village to its inhabitants; to passers-by all are evidence of life's anonymous sameness. Boisterous teenaged boys and laughing girls stroll past old men and women in lawn chairs gathered by worn stone steps. The profusion of delicatessens makes each one indistinguishable from the next. A man walks his dog; the dog shits over the curb, pisses on a fence-encircled tree, and they go home. Cars honk as a delivery boy hustles crates of melons into a restaurant. On the next block a dishwasher is carrying out garbage cans.

Myrtle Avenue eases into Jamaica Avenue, which meets Hempstead Avenue near the eastern border of the city. In Suffolk County—where the commercial buildings are lower, newer, and separated by weedy vacant lots and occasional old houses—that road becomes the Hempstead Turnpike. Number 2071 is in East Meadow; it is a one-story box of white-painted brick, a night spot called, for no particular reason, Jay R.'s Club. The awning is blue with gold trim, and hostess Yolanda Lé Face, who collects two dollars a head for the Sunday-night show, is in red. The present owners are a couple named Ronnie and Barbara who, by featuring live music six nights a week and weekend shows by name acts, strippers, belly dancers, comedians, and magicians, have been doing good business for two and a half years. "All kinds of people come here," said Miss Lé Face, who especially asked for a "thing" over the *e*. "It's a place people keep coming back to, a friendly place."

It seemed so one summer night. About half the tables were filled with young white adults who were neither singles nor married, short-haired nor long-haired, hip nor square. All were out for a good time. Everyone was neatly dressed, but only one girl had a flashy outfit on, and hers, besides showing much bare curved tummy, fetchingly outlined a perky rear end in black stretch nylon. A black and white polka dot scarf served as a belt; its tails twitched like a rabbit's nose. At one table were four couples whose ease of demeanor increased with every round of mixed drinks. The boys backslapped each other and told stories. As their girls set off for the ladies room, they asked them if they needed a dime. The girls were quieter, ignoring the male arm around them as they sat, but dancing close when taken to the floor.

The bar, separated from the rest of the club by a half-partition, was crowded with a jovial crew, and on the bandstand the three members of Just Us—Jeff on guitar and bass, Hank on drums, and Les on electric organ—ran professionally through "Man from Galilee" from *Jesus Christ Superstar* and pop tunes by Three Dog Night and the Carpenters. Each man had his own mike to take his voice through tall speaker columns, and for guitar and organ there were large portable Fender amps. Judging by their accents and the cut of their beige drape suits and frilled brown shirts, they were local boys thoroughly accustomed to working Suffolk's lounge circuit. On every number they got a few dancers; when they closed the first set with Chuck Berry's "Johnny B. Goode," the floor was full of leaping bodies.

Enter Chiffons. Three black women in their mid-twenties—Barbara Lee, Sylvia Peterson, and Pat Stelley—walked in with dress bags over their arms and determined looks on their faces. Barbara and Sylvia both had thick naturals; Pat had her hair in a swept-back style which brought out her high smooth forehead. They got into the dressing room without being noticed. Their guitar player, Doug Ferguson, in jeans and a sloppy shirt, plugged in his Fender Telecaster and gave Jeff, now playing bass, charts for the Chiffons' tunes. They went over them silently, nodding and pointing occasionally, Doug acting out the feeling of unusual phrases and bridges.

They were ready. Hank, the drummer, who had been watching Jeff and Doug from his elevated spot at the rear of the stand, pulled his mike to him. "Ladies and gentlemen, Jay R.'s takes pleasure in presenting the fabulous and exciting *Chiffons!*"

Out came the girls, smiling but not overly sweet, their pace quick and light. They wore black accented with color: Sylvia wore her black top over a long orange African skirt, and Barbara had on an orange rope necklace over her black top and sexy slit skirt. Pat wore only black: the creamy tan of her skin was accent enough. Barbara and Pat took places behind stand-up mikes, Sylvia lifted hers off the stand, stepped forward, and started "Quicksand," a great show opener (the song was the follow-up to "Heatwave" for Martha and the Vandellas on Motown's Gordy label). The Chiffons did every "oooooooh" just right. "Hello," said Sylvia as they finished, "we're the Chiffons, and we're glad to be at Jay R.'s. Our next number will be the Temptations' 'Baby, I Need Your Loving.' " It is a good song, earnest and exuberant, and they belted it. Pat kept a wide smile on as she sang, Barbara was more reserved, and Sylvia was in command. Doug stood with his back to the audience, communicating with Jeff and Hank as they followed his lead through the song. Les sat idle at his organ. Sylvia lifted her right hand, and Doug brought the number to a close.

"Thank you," said Sylvia. "Now we want to go back to 1964 and a song that was a hit for us, 'One Fine Day.' " In the song a girl says that one day the boy who is putting her down will want her back; the message, beat, and unique lift of the melody rise to the high point: *"One* fine da-ay, you're gonna want me for your girl, shoobie doobie doobie doobie doo wah wah." One of the great hits of rock 'n' roll's Top 40, "One Fine Day" was written by Carole King and Jerry Goffin. The song appeared on the Laurie label and was not a huge seller—perhaps half a million—but it is well remembered. Many people who say they never listen to rock 'n' roll can, if their memory is stirred, hum bits of it, smiling as they get the feel of the *"one* fine day." Saturation broadcast for several months nearly a decade ago, it

was then part of America's air and remains a sound of a time.

From that the Chiffons moved to Aretha Franklin's "If I Lose This Dream," and then to some rocking R&B with "Stick Up." The girls never stopped moving, clapping, dancing, leaning to the mike for perfectly timed high shouts, bending away to twirl their hands and bodies in intricate patterns. They did their 1965 hit "Sweet Talkin' Guy," a strong Motown ballad, "Does Your Mama Know About Me?" then "Grapevine" done as Gladys Knight and the Pips recorded it, and their first record and biggest hit, "He's So Fine." This one brought down the house, and before the applause had died away Doug had pushed Jeff and Hank into "Respect." That song was a smash for both Otis Redding and Aretha Franklin; the girls had Jay R.'s crowd where they wanted them, and they socked the song to them: "Give it to me, give it to me, give it to me, I want some *respect* when I get home!" They bowed when done, went off, returned for a final bow, and walked quickly to the dressing room.

"The Chiffons, everybody, a big hand for the Chiffons," called Hank. He extricated himself from his kit and headed for the bar.

The illusion created by a fade-out at the end of a record, like on "One Fine Day" or "He's So Fine," is that the recorded musicians fly away from the listener, on a magic carpet or similar dreamlike device, until their music is too far away to hear. At the end of a live performance only the music disappears into thin air: the musicians and their instruments remain. On record the music cannot disappear because it is captured in plastic. The fade-out creates the illusion that the unseen musicians recede in space or fade away. Their sounds grow dim, but they keep on playing. At the end we can't hear them any more.

Barrett Hansen says that the fade-out—the recording engineer simply rolls down the knob of the pot which controls the volume of original sound fed to the tape depository—was first used on several Leopold Stokowski recordings in the thirties. The pioneering use of the fade-out to replace arranged endings which tradition, but not records, required was rare until the late forties. Ralph Bass remembers his faded end on "Open the Door, Richard" in 1946 as the first he had heard of. The song was a spontaneous creation based on a nightclub comedy act, and Jackie McVea's band had fallen into it as comic relief at the end of a session. Bass dug it, but how to end it? Nothing had been planned, and there wasn't time for a repeat. "Turn 'em off, slowly," he whispered to the engineer, while waving to the band to keep up the groove. The side was a big hit.

In the 1950s and 1960s the fade-out became a distinctive element in rock 'n' roll record making. Before rock, *songs* were hits; with rock, records were hits. Rock hits had songlike verse-chorus structures, but the energy of the records broke through the structure, flowing along a rising curve that reached a climax past the three-quarter point and then, without resolution, simply ebbed away. Music which demands that attention be paid to its own completion divides time into musical and non-musical segments. The fade attempts to do away with that distinction. The perfect fade would let the music slip out of our hearing at the same rate as our attention wandered from it. We stop listening, and the music isn't there any more.

No other music but rock 'n' roll adopted the fade-out until the late sixties (today fade-ins are also common) because the fade violated powerful conventions based on the primacy of live performance. At a concert we see as well as hear. Our eyes tell us that musicians, despite their sonic conjuring power, cannot make themselves vanish. We see them start playing and stop; we see what instruments they are playing at any given moment. In concert musicians usually play pieces beginning to end and, unless on a revolving stage, stop completely before they leave. Whether a musician does or does not involve himself in visual theatrics to support his aural image making, he is, before an audience, affected by optical reality. Musicians have often felt that as a limitation of their powers and have hidden in orchestra pits, curtained galleries, and dark organ lofts. Records blindfold the listener completely. Our eyes are no help in unraveling the web of sound spun for us in a distant studio. We know only what we hear. Do the musicians on a faded record ever stop playing? Perhaps, but we don't hear them. When did the players on a faded-in record begin? We don't know.

Marvelous idea that it is, the fade-out might not have become as popular as it did had it not been ideal for radio. When radio presents music in concert or ballroom format it limits itself to visual conventions. But the beauty of radio, even more than of records, is that it transcends the world of seeing-is-believing. Radio can present listeners with collages of sound from every conceivable source, from all corners of the world and beyond. Being a manipulatable sound-making device, it can be a musical instrument if treated as one. What possibilities! If, however, a frame is put around each spot of sound-color, the collage is divided and ungainly; the medium is subordinated to the units of sound it conveys. The music of a faded-out record, by relinquishing a defined ending, gives up the solitude that goes with independence and can be used in radio as a thread in a seamless blend of sound.

"Col-or *ray*-di-o"—the sung slogan of Boston's WMEX in the early 1960s. Rock 'n' roll radio, beginning with the riotous days of Alan Freed in Cleveland and New York, was a musical development as noteworthy as rock 'n' roll records. Captivating sound—"Don't touch that dial"—was what the radio men were after. The hour-by-hour progression of wake-up shows, soaps, afternoon easy listening, kiddie shows, dramas, and late-night music appealed to many different audiences and moods, but once TV came in, radio could not compete with the newer invention's presentation of the same material. Rock 'n' roll radio did away with such schedules and beamed twenty-four hours of non-stop aural excitement at everybody. It was a Coney Island of the ears, a circus with disc jockey as barker and master of the three rings of music, news, and advertisements. The rings overlapped pretzel fashion. The latest hit faded into the sound effects ("chomp chomp chomp bing bing chomp") of a frantic newsroom. Over that a sepulchral voice read headlines ("The president announced today that in the Gulf of Tonkin . . ."). A

*Pat Stelley*

blast of trumpets, and a chorus of women chanted the station break ("Kay Eff Arr CEEEE, San Fran*cis*co"). At this point the jock could slug in canned maniacal laughter, the roar of a dragster's engine, a second or two of a "Mystery Tune," or any other surprising sound from his bank of tape cassettes and shout over it in his own voice to announce the next hit, the throbbing bass of which was rising as his voice faded away ("doo lang doo lang doo lang"). The master jocks—Murray the K, Wolfman Jack, Arnie "Woo Woo" Ginsberg, the Magnificent Montague, and Cousin Brucie—were masterful, fast, unerringly dramatic, and unusual. Like their colleagues, "Good Guys" at stations across the country, they aroused fanatical and amused loyalty in the hearts of their listeners.

What was called "teen" or "rock" programing, and later "Top 40," became as popular as rock 'n' roll itself, and it is pointless to think of them as fundamentally distinct. From Besman on record producers aimed their product at the listener through the djs; hit records were the ultimate inspiration and attraction of rock 'n' roll radio music. Radio men and record men had different but symbiotic roles in the same business. Aesthetically the concerns of both were the same: the creation of NEW, personally expressive, and overwhelming sound by any means available. Leiber and Stoller put strings and tympani behind the Drifters on "Walking On down the Line"; Jimmy Drake had car crashes on "Transfusion"; David Seville introduced Alvin, the singing chipmunk (thanks to the variable speed tape recorder). Similarly, the stations which played these amazing records had "Name that Sound" contests, mysterious slamming doors, horns, explosions, and disc jockeys who stayed up five days for charitable organizations. "Blasts from the Past" (or "Golden Greats" or "Oldies but Goodies" or "Moldy Goldies") made the entire rock 'n' roll era seem contemporaneous.

Rock 'n' roll radio is now twenty years old and going strong. The color and passion of its music, its parade of hits and misses, fads and foolishness, make a powerful aural spectacle. The freedom and precision of its allusions and the mind-boggling contrasts it creates with brazen juxtapositions are those of a robust and humorous art. Tailored to specifications frankly commercial, it contains all the tumult of the marketplace. Whether we *listen* to it or not, it is there, carried to us by passing cars, or by a kid with a transistor set at his ear, or by a carpenter with a radio beside him at work. We tune in on it spontaneously whenever it attracts us. Rock 'n' roll radio's sound is like that of traffic or birds—music not tied to a time or place but coexistent with us, borne by the air that envelops us, reaching us, as jockey Bob Clayton used to say, "No matter who, what, when, or where you be!"

"That man, he's crazy. He's a crazy faggot, that's what he is!" Pat Stelley covered her mouth with her hand and blushed, but the other girls were shrieking with laughter, and Pat started laughing too.

"We went out on a lot of tours, Dion and the Belmonts, Jay and the Americans, the Four Seasons," said Sylvia, "package shows with all the acts on one bus, city to city, show to show. It was fun and good money, because we never had time to spend anything, but *that* tour, wow." The Chiffons were in the tiny dressing room of Jay R.'s talking about their days in rock 'n' roll show biz, including a memorable experience with one of the era's biggest stars.

"That guy—out of his mind," said Pat. "He was with a whole bunch of faggots, and one tried to kill me. He did, he definitely did. We were the only girls on the tour, going all over the South, don't remember where. One guy'd get on the bus every morning and say, 'Good morning, ladies and gentlemen, or whomever you choose to be this morning.' The straight guys in the band were interested in us, but the fags were interested in them and got mad at us. One night one of them started chasing me, he tore up a whole hotel room. They had to get the police to cool him out. When I saw him on the bus next morning, I said, 'I'm leaving, you all.'"

As the Chiffons tell it, their whole career was an accident, and after a decade of working at it, they don't know if they were lucky or not. Their original lead singer, Judy Craig, stopped performing several years ago; for the remaining three being a Chiffon now means a steady income supplement and the continuation of an adolescent hobby. "We were kids off the block," said Barbara, "Manhattan and the Bronx. We loved all those great groups, Little Anthony and the Imperials, the Drifters, the Dootones or Cleftones or something-tones we'd hear on the radio and see at the Apollo. We sang in the lunchroom and after school for the fun of it."

"Me," said Sylvia, "I didn't like to sing even, but I knew the other girls, and then there was this fellow, Ronnie Mack. He was off the block like us, our age, but he had ideas. He could play the piano so pretty and write sweet songs. He got us together."

"Ronald passed," said Barbara. "He had Hodgkin's disease and lasted just long enough to see us get somewhere. It was like he had to see that, then he could die."

Ronald Mack is not well remembered in rock 'n' roll history. A good-humored musical kid, "too nice," said Sylvia, "to stay around in this world," he wrote songs about his friends and played them at parties and at school assemblies. A prodigy among the singers and players of his set, he had ambitions none of them, however talented, dreamed of. When the girls were still in high school, he somehow scraped up twenty-five dollars and paid for an hour's time in a local studio. "As many songs as we could sing in that hour, we sang," Pat said.

"Just us and him on piano," said Sylvia, "and then he had a demo tape to take around. We, we forgot about it—finished school and got jobs. But Ronald was taking the tape around. He went everywhere, knocking on doors, and all the big companies, Atlantic, Capitol, turned it down."

The only people interested in Mack and his tape were the Tokens. A white male singing group, the Tokens had set themselves up as producers with the profits of their smash hit, "The Lion Sleeps Tonight," an elaborate rock version of the African song "Wimoweh," which the folk movement had made well known in America. They produced "He's So Fine"—Ronald Mack rounded up the girls and got them down to Manhattan's Mirror Sound Studios where they sang the song again—and sold the master to Laurie Records, a small company which could boast only of having Dion and the Belmonts (they also had a still-unknown Petula Clark).

"It started to become a hit about six months after we had recorded it," said Sylvia. "We never expected it. We hadn't seen Ronnie in all that time. Then he came to us and said, 'The record is a hit, selling five thousand copies a day.' " The girls all laughed; ten years later the memory of it—the unbelievable happening to them!—was still a jolt of pleasure.

"We didn't even like that song so much, it was just one of the ones we did," said Barbara, "but it had something that caught people. Everybody said it was those 'doo lang doo langs.' That's what people, when they heard it, couldn't get out of their minds."

> Doo lang doo lang doo lang
> He's so fine, doo lang, doo lang
> Wish he were mine, doo lang doo lang
> That handsome boy over there
> The one with the wavy hair . . .*

A girl sings that she wants a guy; she doesn't know how she's gonna do it, but she's gonna get him, "sooner or later, I hope it's not later." She can't stop thinking about him; we see him through her eyes: "handsome . . . wavy hair . . . soft-spoken . . . shy . . . so fine, so fine." Her artless single-mindedness is her own self-portrait. She is not swooning; she's in love but down-to-earth too. She's not a manhunter, but she's open about her emotions and the possible need for strategem. A young girl in

*Copyright © 1962 and 1963 by Bright Tunes Music Corp., c/o Howard Sheldon, Receiver, 292 Madison Avenue, New York, N.Y. 10017. Used by permission of the Receiver.

love—artists have found nothing in all of nature to compare with her in beauty. Ronald Mack wrote a song for all such girls, found four to sing it, then had their voices cast in plastic as a permanent portrait. The girls sing with open throats, putting the song over with unabashed friendliness. On record, the Chiffons' voices are as alive as at the moment they were caught. That boy is still not in her arms, but she hasn't given up hope. "He's So Fine" is a grecian urn of the ear. How significant are the "doo lang doo langs"? In love, nothings, when sweet, are everything.

When Laurie asked for a name to put on the label, Barbara came up with "the Chiffons." (There have been bird groups—Orioles, Crows, and Flamingos; car groups—Cadillacs and Eldorados; the Marvelettes, Velvelettes, and Ronettes; Temptations, Persuasions, and Emulations; and corresponding to the Chiffons were the Orlons, a three-girl–one-boy group from Philly who also had a string of hits, "South Street," "The Wah-Watusi," and "Don't Hang Up." Their male singer is gone, but the Orlons continue to gig.) "We stopped our daytime jobs then," said Pat, "but we didn't get a band together. We were green. The first show we ever did, it was a record hop. We didn't even have to sing, we just opened our mouths in time to the record. Was I nervous!"

After that first job in Springfield, Massachusetts—a long way from the Bronx for a sixteen year old—the Chiffons went on the road. For five years they were a fully professional, hard working rock 'n' roll act with national appeal. They topped few concert bills but were a drawing attraction on all. They headlined clubs. Show biz respects hits and employs hit makers. One record— four weeks in the spring of 1963 at number one in the charts, and a million-plus seller—made Judy, Barbara, Sylvia, and Pat a *real* group, not kids singing for fun. Yet their success, unlike that of many artists, wasn't connected to their own personal yearning and drive. Nor did it enflame smoldering artistic ambitions. The girls remained girls who luckily had glamorous jobs —which, when it came to it, weren't all that glamorous.

"People wanted autographs, we got interviewed, had our pictures taken so many times, but we got sick of it, tired of the traveling," said Sylvia.

"We could travel now. Our manager, Eddie Martinelli, he offers us the jobs, but we don't take them," said Pat. "A while ago 'One Fine Day' was number one in England—almost ten years after it first came out—and we could have gone to England. We had gone there once and didn't like it. So cold, and we worked and drove so much we couldn't see anything, and it stayed light so late in the summer, we could hardly sleep."

"Work is fun sometimes," said Sylvia, "but then you go out to sing somewhere, and the band is so bad! A bad band can mess up a tune, make it sound like something you never heard before. Know how we smile on stage? Sometimes we're laughing because the band is so terrible."

"We got a guitar player now," said Barbara, "but we haven't always had that. You can have a bass player and drummer too, but that's worries. Worry is the band going to get there on time or show at all. Then rehearse the band. You can rehearse and rehearse a band, and when it's time for the show and you go on, the band forgets everything."

"Of course we don't rehearse so much ourselves," said Sylvia, and they all laughed. "What happens," said Pat, "is one of us says, 'We *gotta* get a new song into the act.' Then we do it. Otherwise we forget it. In a few days we can get a new tune down."

"What takes time is the steps. A good routine really helps put a song over, but it ain't easy to get it so I'm not hand twirling when the others are doing some hip thing!" said Barbara.

As hit number one faded from the charts—"He's So Fine" was the Chiffons' only song to score in the black R&B market as well as in the white pop field—the Tokens started working on hit number two for the girls. The Tokens had a penchant for baroque production, as their records show and as the Chiffons remember. "The money from 'He's So Fine'?" Sylvia grinned ruefully. "That's a long hard story. Like most contracts ours said *we* pay production costs. The Tokens blew thousands in the studio, getting big bands to back us up, doing tracks over and over. They spent our money on their experiments without us knowing it." The girls were all nodding their heads in agreement. "At the time I was sixteen, they were seventeen, we were too young to know. It happened. When the time came for the statement of royalties we had maybe a thousand dollars. Then we saw twenty thousand billed for orchestras, etc. It was pitiful."

"One Fine Day" was their next success. The Tokens didn't have much to do with it. Carole King and Jerry Goffin had completed a ready-to-press master of the tune sung by Little Eva, who had had a hit with "The Locomotion." At the last minute they or Little Eva's management decided against it for her. So King and Goffin went back to the tapes, erased Little Eva's voice, and looked for someone else to sing the track. They found the Chiffons, for whom, all agreed, another "fine" song was, hitwise, the perfect follow-up.

"Carole King came over to the Tokens' studio. She was very nice, very patient," said Pat. "She was well known in the business then, but the public didn't know about her until she started singing on her own records. She showed us the tune, we took it home, rehearsed it, learned it, went in and recorded it, singing along with the band track that was all ready. It was a good hit."

At this point Doug, the guitar player, stuck his head into the dressing room. The sound of Just Us doing the Everly Brothers' "All I Have to Do Is Dream"—it was golden-oldie night at Jay R.'s—came pulsing into the smoky room.

"I think we're gonna get away with an early night," Doug said. "It's only twelve thirty, and they're winding up their act. We'll be able to get on before one."

"You think so?" said Sylvia. Barbara looked doubtful. "Don't count on it," she said. The girls had been in more clubs than Doug: Ronnie and Barbara weren't hurrying anyone out of Jay R.'s ahead of time, and certainly not the act they were paying for. The girls sat patiently as Just Us did "Book of Love"; their years of experience showed in their calm. The room's one light-bulb burned on. Smoke from the girls' cigarettes floated to the ceiling.

"We never picked our own songs," said Sylvia, "never had a thing to say about it. When we had something together we wanted to do, they'd say, 'It's not commercial.' "

"That was their line for everything," said Barbara.

"They got on that 'fine' business, got carried away. Anything with 'fine' in the title, that was for us," said Pat.

"We were always unsatisfied with our material," said Sylvia. "We wanted a chance to show we could sing more than ice-cream tunes. The Tokens were intentionally aiming us at the early-teen pop market. 'I love you, please be my boyfriend.' We felt we were maturing, that stuff felt *stupid*. So we tried to get away from the Tokens, after the third hit which wasn't so big, 'I Have a Boyfriend.' But they had option after option, they didn't want to let go."

Pat broke in. "So we told them we weren't going to record, and then we didn't show up for sessions. One night we're at a club, and a guy stops us as we're leaving the stage, a young guy, we thought he was a fan. He handed us something. It was a summons. We had taken it like fools, our hands open!"

There followed a long court fight. Eventually the girls won, largely because Sylvia was still under twenty-one. Where to go next? In the late 1960s some extremely successful white rock 'n' roll stars were able to dictate their terms to the record compa-nies, but in 1966 a group of black girl singers had next to no bargaining power in Tin Pan Alley. Understanding producers did not flock to hire the contract-breaking Chiffons. The girls did not write songs, produce, or play instruments, nor were they, individually, singers. They were a hit-making singing group and that only. They needed records for their professional existence, but they could not make records themselves. Fans care who sings on a record; in the business, singers are a com-modity used in the manufacture of plastic discs. Nothing better turned up, so the Chiffons took the deal they could get, signing directly with Laurie Records. "Sweet Talkin' Guy," a mellow, lovely song, was the first result of their new start and a medium big hit.

"But we were back doing ice-cream stuff," said Sylvia. "We could record some material we liked, but they only promoted what they wanted to. We did one beautiful Carole King song, 'Hey Baby.' It could have been big, but Laurie didn't think so, so it wasn't." "Teen feel"—that was what producers thought sold records. The innocence which the girls had projected on record was what they had been hired to deliver. As they lost it, they lost their role in an industry which was as fickle as the fashions it profited from.

Six years after "He's So Fine" the Chiffons were no longer contemporary hit makers. Their last contract with Laurie Records ran out, and the company moved on without them. "Once your contract is up with the record company, you aren't connected to them in any way," said Barbara. They had had a good run; to go further, as Sylvia added, they would have needed "the right people, the right material, and money invested." Motown, which prides itself on a family attitude toward its talent, is the only company which has kept alive the recording careers of hit makers for more than a decade. "Laurie, they were so cheap," said Pat, "for our LPs, we had two, they took us to the cheapest place in town to get our pictures taken. Pictures on record covers usually make you look better than you really look. Ours made us look like something out of the *National Enquirer*."

"Show biz, it's all ups and downs," said Sylvia. Waiting for, *needing*, hits had tied the girls to a wearying cycle of hope and frustration. "*We* never knew what made the songs hit records," said Barbara. "We liked them when we learned them and recorded them, but after that we never knew." By 1970 they were in their mid-twenties; Pat is now divorced, but all were then married. An endless grind of one-nighters in increasingly small and remote venues was the only way to keep a full-time career going. None of them wanted it.

They got daytime jobs again. Barbara trained as a hairdresser, got a job in a wig store, and now manages a wig store in a New Rochelle shopping center. Pat is in charge of dry-goods inventory at the Bronx's Montefiore Hospital. Sylvia is a receptionist at St. Luke's Hospital in Manhattan. The jobs require intelligence and responsibility; the girls handle them with ease. Being on stage and out in the world has made them three strikingly modern and capable women. Three years ago they started wearing their hair natural on stage and off, and they have now almost forgotten what a step that was. In clubs they are all business. "Some places, the owners want you to mingle between shows, be friendly, drink with the customers. But you get big smiles and wandering hands that way. So we sing and then stay in whatever cubby hole they have provided for us," said Pat. They make their own decisions, live as they please. They know how to have a good time, and they do. Only Sylvia mentioned future plans: she wants to become a nurse. "That's the profession I should have been in long ago," she said.

Performance dates, channeled through Eddie Martinelli's office, have never stopped coming in. Nothing spectacular—clubs, colleges, high school proms, rock 'n' roll revivals—but enough for four to ten nights of work a month. Their hits have lasted, and they deliver a solid and enjoyable act. They always do "He's So Fine" and "One Fine Day"; the rest of their act they choose from contemporary rhythm-and-blues. They sing with feeling. Their voices are true, their dancing energetic. They don't do ice-cream songs.

It was one o'clock, even a few minutes past. The girls excused themselves to change. In the club the lights dimmed, Hank announced them once again, and they swept out, this time in maroon and gold. They began with "Heatwave" ("Don't understand it, can't explain it, ain't never felt like this before"). The show was basically the same with the addition of two rockers, "Sugar Pie Honey Bunch," and "I Can't Help Myself." They had a groove going, and the whole club picked up on it. Remembered hits drew the big applause—the shouting and the singing along. For everyone there the "doo lang doo langs" and the "shoobie doobie doobie doobie doo wah wahs" renewed stored moments of pleasure. The songs were being sung before our eyes by the girls who until then had only been known—although known intimately—as disembodied voices. We had never seen them before, but their music, recorded and beamed to a world of listeners, was already in our hearts. Sylvia's fist clenched in dramatic defiance.

One fine day, you're gonna want me for your girl!

Pat and Barbara, their hands on their hips, twisted and dipped as they responded, "One fine day, you're gonna want me for your girl, shoobie doobie doobie doobie doo wah wah!"

For Pat, Barbara, and Sylvia the songs are memories too. Before they were Chiffons they were the Sweethearts, the Schoolgirls, the Preteens, and the "G's" in Four G's and a B. They're Chiffons now only on stage. At their daytime jobs their bosses don't know they ever were Chiffons. They tell only close friends. It is easier that way, they explained. When they do know, other people make a bigger deal about it than the girls do, so why talk about it at all? "They'd blame our singing if we ever came in late or called in sick," said Sylvia. They are still friends with Ruby of Ruby and the Romantics, who had a big hit with "Our Day Will Come." She's their only connection with their days as a top group. Ruby grew up in the same New York neighborhoods and went through the hit-record cycle at the same time. She fell in love with a school-teacher from Ohio, and for a time flew to jobs and then back to Ohio. Then she quit, got married, and is now raising a family. Every once in a while they all get on the phone and talk over old times.

"If we had a chance to record again, go for the top again, we wouldn't do it," Barbara had said.

"To us it's a job," Sylvia added. "We were never stars or any of that phoniness. Some groups have disagreements and split up. Not us. When we disagree, we have our say, and then the hell with it. If you got any sense and you got a job, when you get mad at the boss, you don't quit right there. You got to make a living. So you do what you gotta do, cool off, and go back to work the next day. That's how we feel, and we'll keep going that way as long as people like to hear our songs."

Yolanda Lé Face said good night to everyone as they left. She was happy because everyone had had a good time. Traffic on the avenue outside was down to late-nighters, like Jay R.'s customers, going home. In Brooklyn solitary cabs were racing fifteen blocks without stopping for a light. In the morning the avenue would be jammed again.

● In the fall of 1965 the Action were at their zenith, one short step above complete obscurity. For one all too brief moment they had a chance at success. They had a clean R&B-rock 'n' roll sound, drive, and a sense of humor. Londoners by birth and temperament, they were then only a notch or two behind the Small Faces. For whatever reason, they were not graced by fame, and though I heard years later that Reggie King, the lead

THE ACTION

singer, was still in the business producing records, the Action have long since disappeared.

London was swinging in 1965, debutantes were playing with fire in crowded discotheques, the dedicated followed the fashions of Carnaby Street and King's Road, and "New Britain" was the name for the colorful optimism which sometimes broke through the fog of perpetual economic crisis. The Action were part of swinging London though it never swung in their direction. Rolls Royces and baccarat are ever for a few. Reggie, Al, Mick, Pete, and Roger were but rock 'n' rollers, as resilient and slyly game as Sam Weller and their cockney ancestors. Not heroes like the Beatles, Stones, Who, Kinks, Zombies, Hollies, Eric Burdon, or Rod Stewart, the Action remained working class.

When rock 'n' roll reached England, the only people who picked up on it were kids. It did not become a pervasive force until Beatlemania, and, originating as it did in a foreign country, it was a more special phenomenon to its English fans than to Americans, who could take it for granted. In England before the Beatles, to hear rock 'n' roll you had to love it. English fans were ravers. They adored Buddy Holly, yearned for Elvis, and screamed for Gene Vincent. Cults gathered around Chuck Berry. Some bought instruments and got together with friends. This is how the five members of the Action told their story on a rainy October night halfway through the sixties.

*Mick:* For a start we work very hard.
*Reggie:* In the beginning we were called the Boys.
*Pete:* Do you want to go back that far?
*Roger:* Yeah, when we first started.
*Pete:* Actually the last couple records we did came out one day, went in the next.
*Reggie:* Well, we were professional about two years ago with a girl singer. We were called Sandra Barry and the Boyfriends.
*Pete:* What rubbish that was.
*Reggie:* We were thrown together by this sort of big ideas manager.

*Mick:* We was only together two weeks when the record came out.

*Reggie:* Originally before that I was in a small group in a pub, the Vanity.

*Roger:* That's where it all started.

*Reggie:* We broke away from that 'cause we didn't like playing in a pub. We had bigger ideas.

*Roger:* Drunk every night.

*Reggie:* We wanted to get on, so we broke away. I knew Roger could drum, sort of, so we asked him to join. I had been singing since I was pretty young.

*Pete:* You look pretty.

*Al:* You was young and pretty.

*Reggie:* I used to go to the Saturday-morning matinees in the cinema. All the kids used to go. And, of course, when trouble started, they used to get little kids to sing—in front of the mike, you know. And if you were good and they clapped, you'd get an ice cream, and I used to get ice cream.

*Roger:* Every Saturday morning, we used to say, "We want Reggie. We want Reggie."

*Reggie:* So I'd sing. Course I wouldn't get ice creams now. I'd sing silly songs, songs of the time.

*Roger:* It was rock 'n' roll, rock 'n' roll. We was about nine or ten, thirteen years ago.

*Reggie:* Kentish Town, we all lived around that area at the time, tough area, near Hampstead. We were hard kids then. Wore jeans and bumper boots.

*Roger:* Me and Reggie used to go to the Army Cadets, when we was about fourteen.

*Reggie:* Roger fancied himself as a bit of a drummer, used to get biscuit tins . . .

*Roger:* Baked-bean tins.

*Reggie:* . . . and a billiard cue and break it in two, sitting there bap a rappa dappa, and I'd sit at the piano going ching ching ching, making weird noises.

*Roger:* I was self-taught and watched other people.

*Al:* He's got the biggest collection of biscuit tins you've ever seen. Me, on the guitar, it was the thing in those days, everybody was playing.

*Pete:* We just followed suit.

*Al:* I thought it would be a five-minute wonder with me. Me dad bought me a guitar, and never told me, for Christmas, and he laid it over the arms of a chair. I came walkin' in and went to sit down, and he said . . .

*Reggie* (falsetto): "Don't sit down."

*Al:* And I looked around. I was fourteen. It was a cheap one, a Gamadges guitar.

*Roger:* A gas guitar.

*Mick:* Steam.

*Al:* I picked it up, started out on it, then left it for two months, went back to it, and haven't looked back.

*Pete:* I listened to Buddy Holly, the Shadows, Eddie Cochrane, Gene Vincent. No teacher. I bought books with the chords, like the others, played with records.

*Reggie:* You'd bump into friends and swap ideas.

*Roger:* I had a jew's harp when I was three.

*Reggie:* We went professional when we were tired of work.

*Roger:* I worked down at Smithfield's Meat Market, and got fed up, had to start work at four in the morning, so I thought I'd join a group.

*Al:* Reggie and me had started one.

*Reggie:* I used to play with Mick when I was younger, in another group. Then I broke away and joined this group in a pub which needed a rhythm player, and Mick happened to walk through the door with a guitar in his pocket. Then we left the group and saw Roger, who happened to have a set of drums in his pocket.

*Al:* That's how we started up, the four of us with a girl singer.

*Mick:* We was making more in the pub than what we're making at the moment. The Malden Arms in Kentish Town.

*Reggie:* There was always fights in there. We made a pound each night, four nights a week, for two and a half hours a night. Played pop stuff, the hit parade. Rehearsed one night a week.

*Al:* We had regular jobs then, the music was a bit on top of our wages. It helped.

*Reggie* (falsetto): We was rich men.

*Roger:* We got this big ideas manager who used to come down and see us. We just got to talking one night, and he thought we had potential. He liked us. We wanted to get out of the pub, and he talked about turning professional. I thought it wouldn't be worth the time, that we couldn't get anywhere. We had no intentions of getting on to something. He found Sandra Barry, got her because she had had a name as a child star and he thought she could draw people. So we started out.

*Pete:* I knew Mick from working in a music store.

*Reggie:* After a while we found we was lacking a sound, you know, we needed a lead guitar.

*Mick:* We was flopping on jobs cause we needed a bigger sound. Good jobs too, not many jobs, but good ones.

*Pete:* The manager had the gift of gab.

*Reggie:* We were the second group to the Swinging Blue Jeans, thirty-five, forty pounds a night, which is good.

*Roger:* The manager took the lot.

*Reggie:* We were done, we were fiddled, we were rolled.

*Roger:* We managed to get a bit in the end, but not the amount owed to us. We had signed a bit of paper with his name on it. Were owed fifty quid each and got twenty.

*Peter:* That was February, 1964. In four months we broke up because he kept on fiddling us. The girl left too. Had one record, "Really Gonna Shake." Reggie wrote it.

*Reggie:* I've written quite a few, but they're with a publisher that we don't want to be with now. We signed to a publisher as writers, and we don't want to release any through him. He's got the songs we've written, but we won't give him any more because there are publishers a lot better than him.

*Roger:* If we record anything we write, we'll do it under another name. He's got an option for another year; if the record got anyplace, he might take us up on it.

*Mick:* Then we went to Germany. Manager rolled us on that as well.

*Reggie:* We was out of work, didn't have a penny between us.

We went across for about two months, it was seventeen pounds a week apiece. Hanover, Brunswick, month each. Teenage places. Five hours during the week, 8:00 P.M. to 1:00 A.M., seven hours on Sunday, six on Saturday. Seven nights a week.

*Mick:* He sent us over there, speakers and things started to break, the amps, and we needed repairs. We phoned him up and asked him to send stuff over. He said, "Yes, I'm coming over, I'm sending things," but he never came, so in the end we stopped his percentage. The money we stopped we bought speakers with. He left us out there as well.

*Pete:* We had no van.

*Reggie:* Mums and dads had a big whip around between them and sent out a chap with a van to pick us up. The money we should have sent him paid for our fare home, so we came out almost even.

*Mick:* When we come back, we signed up with another crook and had another record out.

*Reggie:* He was a real con.

*Mick:* He had P. J. Proby.

*Reggie:* He took us right, left, and center. A penny here, a penny there. Made a record for Pye, "It Ain't Easy." Me and Mick wrote it.

*Roger:* It came out and went in again.

*Reggie:* I made thirty-three quid on the first record , 7s. 4½ d. on the second. Never knew how they did. Not well enough to get on the charts.

*Pete:* We was promised so much on that record, we was promised on the television shows, and in the end we had one, and that was up in Newcastle.

*Reggie:* We came back from Germany in September, 1964. The record was out in November.

*Roger:* We thought we'd all be comfortably off by Christmas. Nobody did anything for the record. At the time we had two managers, you see, and each manager was blaming it on the other one. Actually it was three managers.

*Pete:* Each manager didn't want to do more than his share.

*Reggie:* We knew there were a lot of jobs around, and we weren't getting any. So we decided to leave, and Kenny the manager was saying, "Oh, there's not much work around anyway," and we knew there was.

*Mick:* It was toward the end of that that we got a residency at the Marquee.

*Reggie:* Then we signed up with another crook.

*Mick:* Not so much a crook, more an ice cream.

*Reggie:* An idiot.

*Pete:* He had all the right ideas, but he didn't have no money or anything like that.

*Reggie:* He's Polish. He'd come up to me with an idea, he'd say, "It's great, great, fantastic," and he'd forget about it in a couple of weeks.

*Mick:* He had another business.

*Reggie:* He used to run this thing on Tuesday nights at the Marquee in Soho. The Who were there then. They wanted a backing group, so we managed to get the job. We did pretty well, actually, for three months. We got a percentage of the gate, started off as nine pounds and ended up as twenty-one.

*Roger:* About 12.5 percent.

*Reggie:* It was more of a prestige thing than the money.

*Mick:* You go there for low money because of that. That gig made the Who.

*Pete:* Our sound, was, well, it was around then, just before we started at the Marquee . . .

*Reggie:* We were still groping for an image and everything.

*Mick:* It sort of came naturally, and we knew that was the sort of stuff we were going to play. We started learning it.

*Reggie:* It's American rhythm-and-blues without the blues, it's sort of rhythm and soul. It's all this reaction music, you know, it's us and the audience, it takes two.

*Mick:* It's American Negro pop.

*Al:* Impressions, Temptations, Martha and the Vandellas.

*Pete:* Almost everybody on Motown. Supremes, Miracles, Marvin Gaye.

*Reggie:* Ena Sharples.

*Roger:* We wanted to get a band sound.

*Mick:* It came naturally. We realized Al and Pete could sing falsetto. Where the records had trumpets we put voices.

*Reggie:* We sort of did scat in harmony.

*Pete:* When we started I was taking lead on the trumpets, but that lost the sound, so instead I'd play chords. Playing chords in the background instead of picking out the tune on guitar, we could save the guitar for a bigger backing, and do the tune with voices and harmony.

*Roger:* Then we got chucked outa the Marquee.

*Mick:* We was taking the limelight from the Who.

*Reggie:* The Who wanted a pony group following them.

*Mick:* They liked it when there was a good crowd and when they were on everybody was watching and when they went off the crowd died out. In the end they were getting a thousand people in there.

*Reggie:* They came to watch us as well.

*Mick:* Their management didn't like it.

*Roger:* When the Who went off they'd sit and wait for us, instead of going out to the pub where the Who went.

*Reggie:* So their manager thought it the wisest thing to kick us out. He was running it there.

*Pete:* We had our own sound. When the Who came on it wasn't such a climax.

*Al:* The way he tried to do it, he accused us of copying them. That was his first excuse.

*Reggie:* The worst thing about that was that it stuck.

*Pete:* We didn't just get kicked out. It built up over time.

*Al:* It started by people saying, "I hear you're leaving the Marquee." We took no notice of that. Then two weeks before the sack, they knocked our money down to a straight fifteen pounds a night, thinking we'd say, "Oh, forget it, we're leaving," but we didn't.

*Roger:* If they'd said "Play for nothing," we'd have played there if we could have afforded it.

*Reggie:* We were low on money.

*Pete:* Then we got Bob Druce as an agent and got jobs all around the country.

*Reggie:* The Polish manager wanted a record, but he didn't have the money for the recording. We wanted a backer, so we went to the Marquee Studio and made some tapes, sent them to Decca. They turned it down. Then George Martin came to see us.

*Roger:* That was Reggie's work.

*Reggie:* This Bob Druce agency had this girl Denise Hall working for them. She got us bookings, and she liked us a lot. (General giggles.)

*Reggie:* Shut up!

*Roger:* Just good friends.

*Reggie:* I was going out with her, like friends, but she liked us as a group, musicwise. She was really plugging us at the agency, working all day calling up people saying, "Book the Boys, book the Boys."

*Al:* Meanwhile we had changed our name to the Action.

*Reggie:* That was her idea. She left the agency to work for us as a publicist. The Pole after a while got broke and couldn't pay her, so we kept her on for 10 percent of what we earned.

*Pete:* She called Martin, phonin' him up, phonin' him up.

*Reggie:* Yeah, she made a nuisance of herself, and he finally came down to see us.

*Roger:* Everybody else had turned us down. We had started at the bottom and worked to the top.

*Pete:* Martin heard us at the Bedford Hotel in Balham.

*Roger:* The Gateway to the South.

*Reggie:* Very pretty there, see the lights turn from red to green, green to amber, back to red again.

*Pete:* Martin liked us, so a week later we went into the studio 'cause he wanted to hear us there. We did "Land of a Thousand Dances."

*Reggie:* We had played it for about three weeks before we recorded it and suddenly thought it could be the one.

*Pete:* Martin hadn't heard it. He had heard "In My Lonely Room," wanted us to do that.

*Mick:* When we walked in we were all depressed 'cause we thought it would be a lousy session.

*Reggie:* It was the most fantastic big studio we had ever seen. [EMI Studios, Abbey Road, London]

*Pete:* We had the song written out on a torn bit of scrap paper.

*Reggie:* I had a sore throat. I thought, "Ridiculous—the top man in the business, and we're all feeling terrible." This chap walked in and said, "Sit down over there," and started fiddling with mikes all over the place, and we were sitting.

*Pete:* It was just an audition, you know. They wanted to hear the tape, and if it was no good, it would have been, "Sorry . . ."

*Al:* We did two songs, the backings with Reggie mouthing the words to keep tempo, and the back-up vocals. Then we had a cup of tea.

*Pete:* Then Martin comes in and says, "First, let's get in tune, shall we?" So we did it all again.

*Al:* But all he really added were some lower harmonies on "In My Lonely Room."

*Reggie:* "Land of a Thousand Dances" he said was too hard on the ear.

*Pete:* But he said he liked "Lonely Room," and "Let's release it," he says.

*Reggie:* We didn't know what was happening, didn't know what time it was. He says he thinks it is very good, and we started talking contracts. We were dazed.

*Roger:* We went up to his office, and he got us out of our old managerial deal.

*Reggie:* The Pole agreed to part with us if we paid him the money we owed him, forty-two pounds.

*Pete:* George Martin paid it, wrote out a check and gave it to us. He didn't know us, only a few hours, that's how much he thought of the record.

*Reggie:* We talked about managers, and he said, "Would you consider Brian Epstein?" And when we all climbed back into our chairs—I did fall on the floor. He approached Epstein about it, played him the record.

*Mick:* He liked it but didn't want to give a definite answer at the moment, but Martin wanted to know, as he was going away for a few days. So Epstein said, "Yes I will manage them as a favor to you, George," but Martin said, "No, I don't want you to manage them unless you're going to push them." He'd have to work for us if he was going to manage us.

*Reggie:* So we turned down Brian Epstein. Put that in.

*Pete:* You can't really. We never even met him.

*Mick:* We met Rikki Farr about then. He owns a club in Portsmouth, a knockout club.

*Al:* One of the best in England for the stuff we play. They go mad for us.

*Mick:* I told that to Nick Jones of the *Melody Maker,* and he put it in his column, "The Raver."

*Al:* Every time we see him we say the London scene is going down.

*Reggie:* So he started managing us. He's like George. Gets things done. Maybe we'll get some TV, but we've been disappointed about that. It's all if they like the record. *Ready, Steady, Go* is the best, but you go on the rest for the plug.

*Pete:* Martin wanted the record out earlier, but then he was going independent from EMI to make his own company, AIR. Rikki was gonna have us raid Radio London in a Chinese junk, get in the national papers that way, but nothing has happened yet.

*Reggie:* Right now we're working an erratic schedule, sometimes five nights a week, other weeks two or three.

*Roger:* We're on "vacation" now.

*Reggie:* We need it after last Sunday. We broke down.

*Pete:* But last week we were at Rikki's flat in Brighton.

*Reggie:* Steak! Steak for breakfast.

*Al:* Birds all over the place.

*Mick:* Rikki's father was a boxer, you know, fought Joe Louis.

*Reggie:* Where we been working most recently is at the Pontiac. We signed for four weeks, then they added four more.

*Mick:* It's a good club, but the trouble is Flynn doesn't have the money to exploit it.

*Al:* He's got good ideas about decorating the place, but as far as booking things, I don't think he has the slightest idea of what he's doing.

*Mick:* Chuck Berry is coming to the Pontiac.

*Reggie:* 'Cause the Pontiac is supposed to be the new in place.

*Pete:* Berry! We saw Bo Diddley, he stood there like a big dummy, even tuned up on stage. Very unprofessional.

*Al:* The Pontiac has the name, but it's gonna go down.

*Pete:* He's put the wrong names in.

*Al:* Nobody wants to see Chuck Berry any more.

*Reggie:* They should, but they don't.

*Al:* I'd say this was a tense time for us. We think the record will do something.

*Pete:* I think it will go well enough to get, you know, fairly well known.

*Roger:* And then the next record . . .

*Reggie:* This record could very well get us in the Hit Parade, put it that way, and if it doesn't . . .

*Roger:* Another one will.

*Reggie:* It gets us a name, known over the country.

*Roger:* Top fifty we're hoping to get.

*Reggie:* If it gets in the top fifty anything can happen.

*Pete:* Once a record is in the top fifty, (snapping his fingers) television programs (snaps again).

*Reggie:* It comes automatic, they come to you.

*Mick:* Martin stated quite categorically, if it misses, he doesn't want to know us.

*Reggie:* That doesn't mean just this record.

*Al:* But it won't go on forever, making records that fail.

*Pete:* If we fail, he's failed as well.

*Al:* He's really keen. He's the first person we ever met in this business who's shown confidence in us.

*Reggie:* Really, really shown confidence.

*Roger:* He's straight, straight as the day is long.

*Al:* He's a really nice fellow.

*Reggie:* He couldn't be crooked—he's too big, it wouldn't pay. But the label is not so good.

*Roger:* We haven't been rehearsing much. As much as we can, it used to be five days a week.

*Reggie:* We haven't been finding material. If you work five nights a week, and mostly you're traveling, you're too tired the next day.

*Al:* Ugh.

*Reggie:* My voice goes all the time. Recently I had sort of a bad cough, 'bout a month ago, and it made my throat sore. I'd be sore before I started. You have to watch those things, like broken fingers.

*Al:* We might be big sometime, as big as we can.

*Reggie:* We're quite prepared to work. If you get to number one, you'll be working seven, eight days a week.

*Roger:* The record is nothing. We're not even worried about the record sales.

*Pete:* We don't count them.

*Reggie:* You get TV, sixty, eighty, a hundred pounds a time.

*Roger:* And it goes up the more you're on.

*Reggie:* And you go straight out to a dance hall the same night, and you earn three hundred pounds, or two hundred, so you're earning money.

*Pete:* Get on the Hit Parade, and your money goes straight to one fifty pounds a night.

*Roger:* I'd buy a yacht with the money.

*Reggie:* Clothes, loads of clothes.

*Pete:* New equipment.

*Reggie:* Yeah; we got good stuff, but it's going now.

*Pete:* We'd get the best equipment money could buy. The PA system, three mikes, and the speakers cost four hundred quid alone.

*Reggie:* Wouldn't get uniforms, just right smart gear.

*Roger:* We got shirts the Pontiac guy had made, one of his good ideas, "Superduperman."

*Al:* I painted stripes on my belt.

*Reggie:* We swap our gear—he wears my shirt, I wear his jumper.

*Pete:* We're getting to be pretty fashion conscious.

*Al:* People notice the clothes, not the person wearing them. So they say, "I've seen it somewhere before, but which one was wearing it?"

*Roger:* We go to some good parties.

*Pete:* Last party we went to, they broke bottles over our heads.

*Reggie:* We got invited to a party, got there after we finished work, and all the beer was all gone.

*Roger:* The people were a bit inebriated, didn't like us coming in. They picked up some empty bottles, and we went out.

*Reggie:* Shattered our egos somewhat. We get to some weird places now and again.

*Roger:* Shocking, shocking.

*Mick:* The kids don't like us in uniforms.

*Reggie:* Some do.

*Al:* We don't want to be like that.

*Mick:* I couldn't play in a suit.

*Al:* If we all dressed the same the way bands used to, I wouldn't play the same, it would affect the way we play.

*Roger:* We can't spoil what we got now.

*Reggie:* We didn't plan how we were gonna look on stage, never got down to it.

*Mick:* One of the reasons the Tamala-Motown groups didn't go over so well when they came here was their American Negro flashy clothes.

*Reggie:* Apart from being Negroes.

*Roger:* That doesn't matter with the hip ones, with the masses it does.

*Reggie:* Being white but singing Negro stuff would go over bigger with the masses, but not the hip people.

*Roger:* Some prefer Marvin Gaye to us.

*Al:* People who like Marvin Gaye like us, but if Marvin Gaye was here, they'd rather watch him than us.

*Reggie:* The stuff we write isn't like Motown. It's sweet, nice music like the Hollies.

*Roger:* It's a cut-throat business. Some of the smaller groups, smaller than even us, that back us, think they're big, think they're it.

*Reggie:* You get to a gig, walk in, and the supporting group, they're all wag around with their noses in the air. You say hello —and nothing. Big groups, they're all friendly straight-away.

*Al:* We're friends with the Who. They speak to us.

*Reggie* (falsetto): Hello.

*Pete:* We're Beatle fans. Like the way they write and play, keep trying for a different sound.

*Roger:* "Yesterday" is my favorite record.

*Reggie:* It's hard to write the Motown stuff.

*Mick:* You can't just sit down and write it.

*Reggie:* It's all based on guitar riffs. Sit down to write something, and it's more complicated.

*Al:* It's soul music, comes from the soul.

*Reggie:* You know, deep down.

*Pete:* It's soul, and we haven't got any.

*Mick:* We can play it though, we couldn't used to.

*Reggie:* Singing like a Negro came naturally to me, never worked on it that hard. About soul, you don't sit down and copy them, you listen to the record and decide whether you want to do it or not, and decide whether it will suit the group.

*Mick:* We have to play it like us.

*Al:* Sometimes we go right through a number, playing it, even after we've finished rehearsing it for three days, we realize it isn't us.

*Reggie:* We listen and write down the words, listen to the record's arrangement, then work it out ourselves, our own ideas, our own sound.

*Mick:* Like the Impressions' number, "Keep On Pushing." It was three-four time, and we was doing dance halls and they couldn't dance to it, so we did it four-four.

*Reggie:* We change it around as we do it.

*Roger:* I change my drumming. I feel a song different after a while.

*Reggie:* In the end it comes around to the way we want it, and then it stays. Half the time we're changing and don't realize it.

*Pete:* It's a good life.

*Reggie:* I enjoy it.

*Mick:* It's better than an ordinary job.

*Reggie:* I couldn't work a nine-to-five job.

*Reggie:* Anything's better than working eight days a week. I don't do it because everybody's looking at us on stage. We don't look.

*Reggie:* That's right. When we're on stage, we're . . .

*Roger:* We get engaged . . .

*Reggie:* You get involved in what you're doing.

*Pete:* When you haven't earned any money in two years, you can't do it without liking it.

*Al:* The sickening thing about some groups, they say, "Oh, if we don't make it, we'll all go back to our regular jobs."

*Mick:* I look bored on stage, but I'm not. It's my image.

*Reggie:* Big moody image.

*Al:* Girls don't go wild over us yet.

*Pete:* We've had our moments.

*Al:* We sent a young lady at the Pontiac the other week. We send her every week.

*Reggie:* The girls, they stand there and dance, look at you, and you look at them, and you give a big hard look, then look away. If you look back later, they'd be waiting there for you to look back. You can play tricks with them.

*Roger:* Yeah, you mess 'em up that way. You work with them to get them to work with you.

*Pete:* We played in a sewer once.

*Reggie:* It was called the Little Fat Black Pussycat Club. It was an old sewer. We pulled up, and I said, "Listen, someone go around to the front," and it was the front. The stage was in the middle, and we was playing to the wall. The people were dancing off to the right. Ridiculous!

*Al:* Fantastic atmosphere.

*Reggie:* There's a lot of crooks in the business.

*Roger:* We play good places though.

*Pete:* We're more a club group than anything else.

*Mick:* We played a strip club once.

*Roger:* It was better watching than playing.

*Pete:* She was changing in our dressing room, wouldn't let anyone look at her.

*Reggie:* Not much drugs. You get pushers around, pills. It's more the audience than the bands. It's pretty rare.

*Mick:* We were playing a club called the Saints when it got raided once. Down the road from the Marquee.

*Roger:* Wardour Street, that's the place where all the clubs are.

*Reggie:* Girls, they get out of school for holidays, and they hang around the street waiting for their idols to come in. Girls come up to you and ask for your autograph, not knowing who you are.

*Roger:* They'd say, "Hey, are you in a group?" We'd tell them no. It's better to tell them that, or they follow you around.

*Reggie:* The Polish manager, he used to run a show-biz football team, where show-biz personalities play for charities. We used to go, 'cause it was a big bully-up, and all the kids would run up saying, "Can I have your autograph," and I felt really embarrassed. So I used to say, "Do you know who I am?" They'd say no, and then I'd say, "What do you want my autograph for?" and they'd all run away.

*Roger:* I went to a football match, and about twenty-five girls came around and said, "Can I have your autograph?" I said, "What for, there's the singer up there," and pointed to my mate. Twenty-five girls came at him.

*Pete:* The funniest experience we had, I have never seen so many girls. They surrounded the van, and we couldn't get out.

*Reggie:* Mass hysteria.

*Roger:* They didn't even know who we was—imagine what it's like when they know who you are.

*Pete:* It would be nice to be famous, just to see what it's like.

*Reggie:* I want to be famous, I don't care what it is like. The

Beatles, they can't go out of their houses, but they have advantages other people don't have.

*Roger:* They go to the clubs, have a good time.

*Reggie:* I'm not really bitter about the class system though.

*Roger:* If I had really wanted to make money, I would have stayed in school and done all that stuff. I wasn't interested in money then, all I wanted to do was leave school. Went to Havistock Secondary Modern.

*Al:* We're all ice creams as far as that is concerned, idiots.

*Reggie:* Can't read music, maybe a single line. I used to write down the top line. The easiest way to learn a tune is with a guitar and singer. We've learned a lot of music by playing.

*Roger:* I play the guitar a little. Sang when we were in Germany. Once dressed up as an Arab. Involved in the music, hah. I would sit in Germany and play with a book by me side, read while I was playing. Mick would come back and chat with me.

*Reggie:* I'd completely forget I was singing. Really. Sometimes I hold my finger in my ear so I can hear myself because it's so loud.

*Roger:* It looks good as well.

*Pete:* It ought to be a gun. When we get really famous we'll employ someone to stand there with a finger in Reggie's ear.

*Roger:* He got his style studying monkeys at the zoo, jumping about.

*Reggie:* I watch people that dance and dance the same as them. That's what I'm doing sometimes, what people are doing on the floor.

*Pete:* We're mods, sort of.

*Reggie:* A mod is more smart, with it, dresses better than a rocker.

*Roger:* They're so nice, mod girls: short hair, big blue eyes, kinky clothes.

*Reggie:* We don't call ourselves mods, we call ourselves individualists.

*Pete:* In between.

*Mick:* Mockers.

*Roger:* I'd vote Conservative if I voted. The Conservatives are the better of the worse.

*Reggie:* We live with our parents, couldn't afford to live anywhere else. If it hadn't been for our parents we'd have been packed up, dead, finished by now.

*Al:* They say they like the music, but I don't think they understand it. They don't make fun of it.

*Reggie:* I've got a couple of sisters who are fairly modern. They come and watch us and rave about us.

*Pete:* We've got a fan club. Two girls, Judy and Pat, run it.

*Al:* They're clever about the membership cards. They started the numbers at about sixty, so everyone who gets a card thinks there are more people than there actually are. Costs five bob to join. The girls in it are about sixteen.

*Reggie:* School was sick, too much discipline. The uniform, that's the biggest thing of all. You have to wear a uniform in English schools. When you're about sixteen, and you're mods or trying to be fairly modern, you look so silly in a blazer and a school cap. We all left about fifteen.

*Roger:* One time I knocked a cop over. I was on a scooter, he was on a scooter. He did a U-turn, I was coming the other way, smash. His hat was rolling on the ground. Hah!

*Reggie:* You know, if I made a lot of money, I'd invest it.

*Roger:* I'd become partners in a club with my friend Gary.

*Pete:* I'd get married. (General laughter)

*Al:* I'd become a beachcomber.

*Mick:* I'd stay in the business and manage somebody.

● Carl Perkins was brought up poor on a tenant farm in the state of Tennessee. They had no electricity, and when the battery ran down, the radio didn't work. Yet when he got his first good guitar about 1950, he bought an electric guitar, a Les Paul model manufactured by the Gibson Company in Kalamazoo, Michigan. This guitar had six strings, a finger board, nut, and bridge, but otherwise was markedly unlike any guitar known

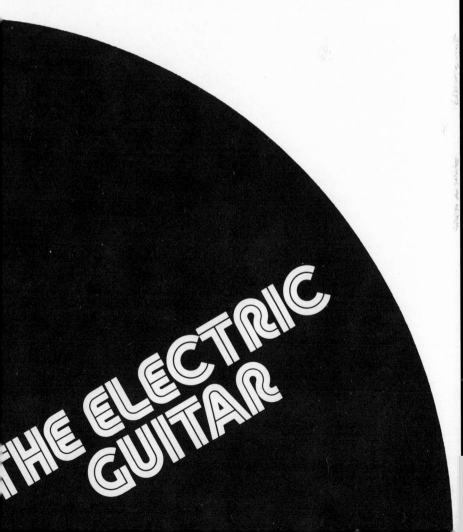

THE ELECTRIC GUITAR

more than a decade earlier. It was a "solid-body" electric, designed at Gibson to specifications set by Les Paul, a guitarist who later had a series of hits with his singing partner, Mary Ford.

Before electrics most guitars had eighteen or twenty frets; only exceptional players ventured freely above the twelfth (octave) fret. The Les Paul's neck was longer, twenty-two or twenty-four frets, and a scoop cut out of the body below the neck allowed comfortable playing above the sixteenth fret. Most peculiar, the body of the Les Paul was a solid piece of wood. An acoustic guitar carries the vibration of the strings through the bridge to a supple sounding board and into a box artfully designed for the mellowest reverberation; this guitar was built not to reverberate. Played unplugged it could deliver only the low and tinny sound of the twanging strings. Since then guitar makers have constructed solid-bodies of plastics and concrete which are deader than wood, but a Les Paul is dead enough.

The acoustic—string and wood to air—sound of a solid-body is purposely minimized. What is important is the guitar's ability to generate electricity. Beneath the strings, near where they are plucked, is a box of small permanent magnets, one for each string, set in a row and wrapped with many coils of fine wire. This is the pick-up; on the Les Paul and on most electric guitars there are two and even three pick-ups, each sensitive to different tonal qualities. The pick-up, says Jack Darr, author of *The Electric Guitar Amplifier Handbook,* could better be called an "electro-mechanical transducer." It is "the device that converts the motion of the guitar strings into electrical signals."

About 1830 American Joseph Henry and Englishman Michael Faraday discovered that a magnet could induce an electrical current if the magnet's field moved. Wave a magnet near a coil of wire, and current proportional to the degree of movement will flow through the wire. In the electric guitar the magnet does not move; the guitar's strings do. Slightly magnetized by their proximity to the pick-up's magnets—though not close enough to have their movement significantly affected by them —the strings, vibrating through the permanent magnets' field, keep the field moving. Current, pulsing like the string, flows through the coil. A sharp stroke across a six-string chord creates about one fourth of a volt of electricity.

This electrical signal, writes Darr, "will be a duplicate of the physical motion of the string. The physical motion is the pitch of the string or the musical note it makes when plucked. The electrical signal is the same frequency as the musical note, and all that is necessary is to amplify it as much as is desired." Each pick-up, however, makes its own version of a duplicate, and there are many different kinds of pick-ups. "The magnetic pick-up doesn't reproduce string sound perfectly," said Dale Frybarger of Oakland, California's Magic Music Repair. "It was first used because it was cheap. It does get the frequency right, but the wave pattern of the electrical signal on the oscilloscope doesn't look like the wave the string makes. The harmonic overtones are all different. But guitarists *liked* the sound it told the speaker to make, so it became popular."

The strings and pick-up generate that quarter volt even when the guitar is not plugged into an amplifier. The wall current does not reach the guitar; the two currents meet in the amplifier. The guitar's signal is strong enough to impose its pattern of fluctuations upon the larger wall flow; that in turn powers the amplifier. The amplified signal passes through the coil around the magnet of the speaker cone; this second electro-mechanical transducer, reversing the effect of the first, creates a sound image of the electricity passing though it. Thus the "sound" of Carl Perkins's Les Paul, and all similar guitars, exists first as electricity. The guitarist and guitar make electricity; the amplifier and speaker turn the electricity into sound. The music comes out of a motionless box which does not need to be close to the guitarist.

Since the first time a guitarist taped a mike to his axe, players have sought ever more complete electrification. Many of the first pick-ups were homemade from telephone receivers. The

Rickenbacker Company of Santa Ana, California, made the first popular line of electrics in the 1930s, but they were "hollow bodies," that is, built like acoustic guitars. With the solid-body there was no longer any pretense of amplifying the sound of a traditional guitar. A new instrument, fashioned from an ancient one, had been born. Most of the pioneers in the development of the electric guitar are unsung; guitarist Merle Travis and a few others make disputable claims to its invention. C. Leo Fender, founder of the Fender Instrument Company, Fullerton, California, was its Henry Ford. In 1948 he brought out the Telecaster; its success continues today. By the mid-fifties good solid-bodies were available from Montgomery Ward, and like the piano stores and woodwind repair shops already dotted across the country, there grew up a specialized trade which supplied the needs and whims of electric musicians.

A guitar makes a man a band; its history, which reaches back to Spain, Greece, and Africa, has been written by wandering minstrels and passionate gypsies. Men who loved their guitars as much as they loved women, the great guitarists have been expressive individualists, proud of the independence their instrument gives them. Many have been singers of their own songs: the guitar serves the solo singer as well as the piano and is far more portable. The guitar has a "serious music" tradition as well, but it is never more at home than on the back porch or streetcorner, in the company of the harmonica, the humble kazoo, and a bottle of wine. In this country and century, when the man with the guitar is white, he's called a cowboy or country singer, and he plays hillbilly, mountain, western, or shit-kicking music. If he's black, he's a bluesman. The labels are misleading; Jimmie Rodgers, Robert Johnson, Leadbelly, Woody Guthrie and Hank Williams shared much.

These men and their fellow innovators of the twenties, thirties, and forties made the guitar an enormously popular instrument in America. Because simple strumming over three or four basic chords can bring to life a vast range of songs, many took up the guitar just so they could sing "You Are My Sunshine,"

"Goodnight, Irene," and "This Land Is Your Land." Some of these amateurs became professionals; the guitar was indispensable to blues and country music. Nowhere else did it have so strong a place. It was not used much in classical circles, and while many dance and swing jazz bands included rhythm guitarists, they were seldom audible above the featured brass and saxophone sections. But by 1950 nearly all professional guitarists had gone electric. Electricity gave the guitar a chance to solo in the otherwise acoustic jazz or pop band. Guitarists in swing ensembles retained the soft rhythmical style of the pre-electric days, playing exotic chords and petallike scales on their hollow-body electric guitars.

Where the guitar had always been more basic, the electric guitar spoke more strongly. Bluesmen played their new electrics—mostly with semisolid or solid bodies—with characteristic intensity and at high volumes. The electric guitar brought the same sudden modernity to country music that electric power had brought to rural life. Even most guitarists who matured before 1950—from Django Reinhardt to Howlin' Wolf—made the switch from acoustic to electric. The generation that followed them grew up and learned to play with electric sound. They did not have known techniques to transfer or modify; their musical ideas were as uncharted as the sonic territory their fingers were eager to explore. A breakaway group of young country musicians, excited by electric blues, started turning on the juice just as a new generation of bluesmen were doing the same thing: this was rock 'n' roll.

My first knowledge of the electric guitar came from an older brother who, returning from a high school dance, said someone in the band had a crazy-shaped instrument with knobs on it that could make an incredible variety of sounds. He didn't know what it was; it was like nothing else he had ever seen or heard. Electric guitars did look different. The gleam of the brass, the golden-brown lacquers of the violin and cellos, and the silver and ebony of the woodwinds were as well known as their sounds. To this traditional spectrum electric guitars introduced screaming pinks and chemical aquamarines in thick layers of shiny plastic paint. Chrome and rhinestones were common. There were knobs, switches, and a wire that led to a black box with more knobs, switches and one small red light. The shape of other instruments determined their sound, and vice versa, but the solid-body's box, freed of acoustic responsibility, could be any shape. Electric guitars were shaped like bullets, arrows, lightning bolts, G clefs, miniature guitars, and violins. The Stratocaster's fluid form, designed by Leo Fender and Freddy Tovares, suggests both wave and flame. "Put a pick-up on a two-by-four, screw strings into it, you got an electric guitar," says one engineer. Many kids did just that, making custom axes as fancy as custom hot rods.

If possible, electrics sounded more unusual than they looked. It was years before I put together what my brother saw with the name "electric guitar," more years until I realized that this instrument produced many of rock 'n' roll's distinctive sounds. The electric guitar did not always dominate—piano, sax, and organ led many bands—but it often did, and it was seldom completely absent. Its sound was sharp, insistent; it could cut through other sound, remaining recognizable even when surrounded by blended instruments. The electric guitar could be played very, very loud, and even when not overwhelming it seemed to penetrate the listener in a new way. It could vibrate the eardrum and the whole body. The nature of the sound was strange and, if for that reason alone, involving. Some people hated it, others felt about it as they felt about abstract art: a modernistic cheat on eternal verities by artists who couldn't paint (or play) better than donkeys. Bill Haley's rambunctious "Shake, Rattle, and Roll" sounded like the rattling of a million tin cans to me in 1955; no wonder some people called it trash. Those who loved the sounds didn't care what anybody called them.

You have probably worked a radio and record player; you may never have touched an electric guitar. That is easily remedied. There may well be a friendly electric musician

nearby; if not, there is probably a music store where the clerks allow the curious to experiment with the guitars on display. So, plug it in and turn it on. Be generous with the volume. As you move your fingers into place to make your first sound— boiiinnng! You brush a string by accident with your sleeve, and out comes a startling blast. Run a fingernail up and down the fattest string—a jet takes off. Fret a thin string and wobble your fretting finger—you could be B. B. King. Switch back and forth between the pick-ups: high frequencies appear and disappear. Hit a note, hold it, then roll the volume knob back and forth; hear the tone fade and return. Perhaps the guitar has a tremulo arm. Wobble that. If the amp has vibrato or reverb, try them. Try a fuzz box and a wah-wah pedal too. Enjoy yourself and the sounds you make.

I did, and now I have a Fender Stratocaster, number 68621. The finger board is black; the body is painted white, but chipped spots indicate it was once a sunburst. At $150 it was an offer I couldn't refuse myself. The homemade speaker and raggedy amp that came with it have worked only sporadically, but many times I have gotten loose on it, completely carried away by the pleasurable sensations of its sounds.

The sound of my acoustic guitar is at my fingertips. Its vibrating body is next to mine. The sounds, made by wood, steel, brass, and flesh, are intimate, as close around me as the glow about a candle. I make the sounds in the same way I push this pen. How do we know how much effort it will take to break a twig or lift a cup? We know, that's all. Similarly, I know what is going to happen (sort of) when I strike the strings of the acoustic guitar. My actions and the sounds they make have the same correlation that I know from a trillion muscular acts. The mechanical action of the electric guitar, however, is transduced into electricity by the magnetic pick-up. It dies as sound, becomes electricity, and is reborn again as sound projected from a black box. It returns from its brief grave in recognizable but totally altered form. The mechanical correlation is still evident—a "hard" stroke returns a "hard" sound—but the sound might be a squeal or a moan or a jumble of squeals and moans. Just as toy magnets can defy in amusing ways the rules that govern ordinary matter, these sounds, made by magnets, play games with our expectations of what action will create what result.

Once when walking in the woods at night, my friends and I came to a grove of overhanging trees. We stopped for a moment to talk and look about, and put our lantern down. When we looked up, we saw our shadows cast huge on the leaves and branches sixty feet above our heads. We found that if we were close to the lantern our shadows were immense; when we danced away a bit they shrank down to life-size in an instant. We played with our shadows for a long time. It was fun projecting and responding to our own images greatly amplified, playing with the relationship of action to image. Everything we did changed our position relative to the trees and lantern, and that position governed how and how much the image was amplified. A hand's shadow was the shadow of a hand if held near a tree trunk and far from the lantern; wave it near the light, and it became a five-headed giant looming far above us.

Playing the electric guitar feels like that. You sense that the relationship between action and result is not that of Hume's colliding billiard balls. As our enlarged shadows leapt twenty feet in response to our moving a few inches, the amplified sound can return an ominous growl for a feathery touch. The guitar and amp create an electrically projected sound image. "Playing an electric guitar is like having your own radio station," said a musician friend. Or a TV station: what television is to the eye, electric sound is to the ear.

Imagine looking at someone and then looking at a TV image of him. The two look alike; if it's Bill in the flesh, he's Bill to you on TV. Yet on screen he is small, grey, and fuzzy, in close-up or perhaps in long shot; the screenview could change angles, change the background, make Bill disappear. Even if the image of Bill is like your view of the real Bill, the quality of attention paid to each is different. The screen of pulsing lines is fascinating; we think we are used to TV, but the awe of its magic will last centuries. You see Bill on TV as you never saw him before. Your view is the camera's; hidden in its "dark room" you peep through the lens. You see Bill as broken up into electrical signals and then reassembled into a screen image. Look again at Bill in person. What is the difference between the two? A process of electro-mechanical transduction.

Watching yourself on the TV monitor and manipulating that image to suit yourself is like playing an electric guitar. The Fender is, in a sense, easier to play than an acoustic guitar. The strings are thinner, lighter, and set close to the frets, making what guitarists call "the action" fast and easy. Playing an instrument, however, is not only finger motions, but making sound.

The sound an instrument makes indicates how it is to be played. Since it must be played to sound, the sentence sounds paradoxical. The experience it describes is not. A musician moves his hands over his instrument. As he feels his arms swinging, fingers pressing and releasing, he hears the sound the instrument makes in response. That sound guides his hands. Musicians often speak of music being in instruments and only released by them. Others say their instruments teach them. Music is a delicious hand-instrument-ear-hand feedback cycle. If a musician likes the sounds he makes, he follows them, his hands striving to caress his instrument and his ears ever more expertly. He learns by repetition with concentration—though, if he is learning, he never repeats. A musician is always listening to himself and responding to what he hears. Gesture—sound—gesture.

On the electric guitar, however, there are two steps of electro-mechanical transduction between gesture and sound. What gestures will suit this transformed sonic response? Only ones as transformed as the sound itself. If the fingers, indeed the whole body, are reacting constantly to aural impressions, they have a whole new job when the ear is lapped by waves of electrical sound. Change the heard sound and the playing must change if it is to be music. The Fender feels fast, the action is slinky, not only because of string, neck, and fret relationships, but because that is how my fingers interpret the sounds coming from the amp. Transducing mechanical into electrical energy seems to take the work out of playing: "It feels like an electric typewriter," said one musician. The vastly increased volume sensitizes the electric guitar by allowing sounds and textures which on an acoustic guitar are nearly inaudible—finger squeaks and buzzes—to contribute strongly to the music. The amplifier's ability to sustain tones far longer than the richest-sounding acoustic suggests gliding movements to the fingers. Because the sound returned is not mechanically commensurate with the energy expended, playing electrically is like semiweightlessness. Steps become jumps, jumps become leaps through graceful slow arcs. John Lee Hooker said it felt "silky." It does.

The electric guitar does not have only one sound. The piano was a marvel in 1800 because it could play loud and soft. Every quality of amplified tones can be manipulated. Even one's choice of guitar and amplifier can make a huge difference in the sounds created. The electric guitar has limits, but they are not the mechanical ones of oboe, horn, and trombone. The guitarist makes electricity first, and then he can shape it as he wishes before it becomes sound. The process of transduction, the flux state between stroke and sound, can be played as my friends and I played the relationship of lantern, tree, and shadow. One plays the guitar *and* the electricity. Adjusting the volume of an amp—and deciding whether to have a big or small amp—is not like going from pianissimo to fortissimo because one changes the amplitude of projection without necessarily changing how one hits the strings. A quarter turn on the volume knob could add the equivalent of a bank of violins; switching to the treble pick-up is an instant brass section. "Do I want this music to sound like a marimba or a symphony orchestra?" Electricity gives an instrument that range.

But even comparisons with acoustic music are misleading. Despite its strength, even the magnificent symphony orchestra cannot match the power potential of the electric guitar. Amplification brings a new scale to the relationship of musician to listener, as different from the acoustic scale as architecture from sculpture. A string quartet plays chamber music; electric quartets, even trios, can play stadium music. Gigantic audiences are common in rock 'n' roll because electricity made such massive concerts possible, and rock 'n' roll musicians play music that moves multitudes. The electric guitar, like recording and radio, has demolished sound barriers higher than the walls of Jericho.

What I have written goes for any electrical instrument. There are now pick-ups for most traditional instruments, and a wide variety of electric organs and synthesizers are available. Yet so far the electric guitar has held a particularly important place. Mass-manufactured before any other electric instrument because it was popular, it was loved because, however changed, it still held the age-old appeal of the guitar. Transduction in no way diminished the sympathetic clarity with which a guitar can give aural expression to movement. The same nuances of stroke bring out the same shadings of tone which generations of musicians and listeners have proven on acoustic guitars to be hypnotically communicative of idea and emotion. The electric guitar attracts the fierce individualists who have always loved the guitar, and they have explored its world of sound like musical Magellans.

The electric guitar is the instrument symbolic of rock 'n' roll, the most popular of electric musics because like its symbol it felicitously combines the known and unknown. The striking qualities of much modern jazz and modern-classical music comes from daring innovations in harmony and tempo, the abandonment of "melody" and theme, and the determination of composers and musicians to free their music from all forms whether consciously or unconsciously imposed on the flow of sound. The rock 'n' roller is more accepting of tradition. Love songs are his specialty, and their content and his intent have not changed a whit since the first troubadour. His language is vernacular, his comedy is as broad as his tragedies are dire, and to succeed he must have the common touch. Often only slightly schooled in music theory, he can hit upon unusual harmonies when they serve the pragmatic and melodic ends of his song. The blues are his meat, pop and country progressions his potatoes. The same C—F—G—F—C sequence is the heart of "La Bamba," "Hang on, Sloopy," "Louie, Louie," and "Like a Rolling Stone." Songs with the C—A-minor—F—G progression are a whole genre of rock 'n' roll.

Most rock departs little from conventions well understood by its audience. What must always be "unique and different," said Ralph Bass, is the *sound*. To achieve striking sounds a rock guitarist can take familiar chord progressions, and color them in the most dramatic tonal hues. Transduction puts at his finger-tips the power to alter all the sound qualities of a note while keeping the same pitch. Since his range of timbres is virtually unlimited, he can play the same old song and transform it at the same time. "Electronic music," which strives for abstract sonic experiences unrelated to previously known musical associations has only slowly gained adherents. Rock 'n' roll, as graphic as the comics about the human condition, has gone straight to the hearts of millions. It is extraordinary music because it electrified the most common music of its day.

There have already been many fine electric guitarists in rock 'n' roll; some I have already mentioned. Memphis' Scotty Moore and Steve Cropper, who played with Elvis and Otis Redding respectively, are best known as studio musicians. Freddy King and Lonnie Mack have had an enormous influence on other guitarists without developing wide followings. The reclusive Link Wray is known only for one epic hit single, "Rumble." Curtis Mayfield is a fine guitarist but is best known for his song-writing, just as the raucous drive of John Lennon's guitar is taken for granted while debates rage about what his songs say. Albert Collins and Buddy Guy are fine bluesmen one genera-tion younger than John Lee Hooker and B. B. King.

Some electric guitarists have become stars of a magnitude that musicians seldom reached before rock 'n' roll. The guitar has always been considered a sexy instrument; electrified and played by a handsome young man, it can be devastating. Chuck Berry and Bo Diddley—I need say no more about what they can do. Michael Bloomfield learned his trade on Chicago's South Side with harpist Paul Butterfield and has since played in many bands and settings. Peter Townshend of the Who and Jerry Garcia of the Grateful Dead have styles as open and friendly as their talkative personalities. The richness and sensitivity of George Harrison's guitar was much of the Beatles' appeal. Rolling Stone Keith Richard plays with stinging intelligence and heart-stopping verve. Eric Clapton imbues everything he plays with a romantic lyricism that could make a statue swoon.

We were lucky who saw Jimi Hendrix play. That man could *move*. As his body danced he brandished his guitar like a flashing sabre, and on its neck his fingers swooped and dove like falcons. His courage, his swashbuckling humor, and his evident pain all contributed to his impulsive grace. Musically he was a dynamo. From the tower of amps behind him came torrents of sound, angry bursts, long curving whines, seductive patches of melodic calm followed by typhoons of savage force. It was often frightening to listen to what he had to say. He knew the blues to the bottom, his rhythms were pure funk, and his singing always persuasive, whether dramatic or conversational. He usually played a Fender Stratocaster. What he did with it is perhaps the most exciting indication yet of what the electric guitar makes possible. Jimi Hendrix was also an excellent record maker, and his LPs display his playing to the full. They repay countless listenings. "Can you hear me sing my song to you? You better hold up your ears, baby!"

● It was a night of nights. Tower of Power set the mood: "You got to funkify," and then King Curtis *and* his Kingpins *and* the Memphis Horns *and* Billy Preston, and after that, Aretha Franklin for an hour and a half, and *then* if your soul can stand it, *Ray Charles and* Aretha, and *all* of the above on one stage gathered, rocking, reeling, rolling, and *tumbling* with the dark spirit of music. It was Sunday, March 7, 1971, the excited eve

of the Ali-Frazier fight, at the Fillmore West in San Francisco. The moment was recorded forever on inch-wide magnetic tape and is available on disc and tape as *Aretha/Live at Fillmore West*. It happened simply.

Aretha was closing her third and final show, leading out of "Dr. Feelgood," as she had on the previous two nights, into a long "yeah"-saying call and response with the crowd; then slowly, as if she were building a sermon, she began "Spirit in the Dark." This song Aretha made the title tune of a record; it suggests that a good cure for whatever ails you is to cover your eyes with one hand, cock the other hand on your hip, and wait until the spirit in the dark comes pulsing inside you and you are dancing and feeling good again. Try it sometime. This night she spread it out forever, then walked off the stage, but came back with Ray Charles on her arm. She led him carefully to the microphone, sat down at the piano, and the song went on. Ray stood beaming, then, encouraged by Aretha, started to sing. The band soul-stewed as never before, the whole crowd boogied, and Ray and Aretha traded shouts, licks, breaks, jumps, and howls, suggesting that everybody get, keep, feel, figure, and cherish that spirit.

It didn't stop. We danced, clapped, hugged, kissed, and finally wept, sweating, eyes open and closed, arms above our heads— and they sang. Aretha found Tower of Power's lead singer and danced with him. She got Ray to sit down and play. Play he did, dazzlingly. In perfect duet, each seemed more individual than ever: Ray a more weathered and older spirit, Aretha a brown blossom, unquenchably feminine youth. Ray's heavy head is touched with grey, Aretha's skin is as clear as a Polynesian's. She was a girl beside him. Their selves seemed commingled.

Finally Ray went off waving to the crowd, leaving Aretha to close her own show. She sang a soft song about reaching out your hand to a friend—"making this a better world if you can." She bowed to all sides, spoke thanks to the band and to the crowd. She said goodbye, goodbye, goodbye. "I love you, I love you." She was gone. The lights went up.

Moments of perfect beauty are brief, impossible to repeat, and ultimately inexplicable. I did that night feel joined in musical-spiritual exultation with Ray Charles, Aretha Franklin, and several hundred other humans. I cannot say how or why. The moment, part of sluggish time, was instantaneous and spontaneous, and seemed to transcend and illuminate the confluence of processes, large and small, which created it.

Aretha Franklin is now thirty. Music has been her life all her life. A performer since childhood, a professional since her teens, a success for nine years, and a star for six, she is the most successful black woman singer ever. Dutiful daughter of the Reverend C. L. Franklin, a preacher who has recorded sermon LPs for Chess, Aretha first sang gospel. She was not yet twenty when she struck out on her own, determined to be a star. For several years she sang and played piano in the supper clubs of Manhattan, recording ballads for Columbia. As she and her listeners began to recognize her talents, they realized she was too fiery for those cool musical settings. Atlantic's Jerry Wexler wooed her, signed her, and put her together with the company's most dependable rhythm-and-blues hit makers. Her first Atlantic single, "I Never Loved a Man the Way I Love You," was an instant smash. So was "Respect," which had also been a hit for Otis Redding; he said gallantly that Aretha had topped him.

At twenty-six Aretha was the Queen of Soul, on the cover of all the magazines, every ambition fulfilled beyond expectation. Her crown, though proffered in apparent tribute, was heavy and hollow. It drove her to drink and demanded as its price an unqueenly slavery to the hit machine of "the charts." Aretha did her best—two handfuls of million-selling singles and four smash LPs in less than two years—but she couldn't keep the inhuman pace. Her marriage fell apart. The "Natural Woman" of 1967 found that "Eleanor Rigby" fit her mood in 1969. She recorded and performed erratically; her popularity and sales suffered. Cynics readied their I-told-you-sos, pointing out that she was falling back on pop tunes like "This Girl Is in Love with You" rather than surging with the R&B which had made her famous. Then she had a hit with the plaintive "Call Me"—not quite a million, but big. Atlantic released *Aretha's Gold,* which summed up her early years. She remarried happily, let her hair go natural, defended Angela Davis as a beautiful black woman, and in 1970 put out *Spirit in the Dark.*

This album, with Aretha shrouded in darkness on the front and looking expectantly into the light on the back, is an absolute triumph, a creation of a strength and grace that few artists ever achieve. Aretha Franklin's voice has always been as supply brilliant as brook water, its expressive clarity always magical. Yet until *Spirit in the Dark* she was a young woman artist moving in a world directed by middle-aged white men whose smiles did not disguise their power. While they needed her voice to make the product they sold, they, not she, determined the essential limits of the product. In 1967 Aretha worked within those limits. She knew no other possibility. All she did know was that she could sing. "My music is me," she said in an interview for a news weekly, "but I'm not sure what that is." Her voice could bring fame, jewels, and white fur. She worked hard like a good girl, quelling her shyness and doing what she called "the uphill thing."

*Spirit in the Dark,* more mature musically than anything she had done before, was a dramatic declaration of independence. The generosity of her self-delight illuminates every song. "Hopes up to the skies," "nobody gonna turn us around," "think I got a winning slip," "I'm pullin' on in," she sings. Five of the twelve tunes she wrote herself; the rest she chose boldly from the hits of bluesmen Jimmy Reed, and Kings, B. B. and Ben E. She makes them all hers. Not once does the band or strings cloud her presence. She plays the piano as she never played it before, striking the keys as hard as Thelonious Monk. The background vocalists, singing arrangements she created, do not just underpin her fervor, they complement it as subtly as perfume.

With this record Aretha Franklin seemed to have become an entirely new artist, if not a whole new person. Her position had

not changed, nor had the soul show-biz limits dissolved. Yet it began to be clear to her that it was no longer necessary to act as others wished her to act. She cut another album, unreleased at the time of the Fillmore concert, which she titled *Young, Gifted, and Black. Spirit in the Dark* was selling well but had not won back the huge audience she had had three years before. So she decided to mend fences and in the winter of 1971 began appearing outside the coliseum circuit to which her Queen of Soul–size fees had driven her. She wasn't playing clubs exactly, but she did go out after an audience. She scrapped the ponderous Donald Townes orchestra, which had accompanied her in concert, in favor of tight combos of rhythm-and-blues studio musicians—often the same men who had accompanied her on record.

The Fillmore weekend was one of a series of promotional dates: on others Aretha was the star of a record-industry convention, and played the Apollo and Fillmore East and some benefits. How much of this she personally planned I don't know. Bill Graham and Atlantic's Jerry Wexler worked out the Fillmore arrangements. The main obstacle was Aretha's own business advisor Ruth Bowen, head of Queen Booking, one of the biggest and most conservative black-run management companies. Mrs. Bowen thought the Fillmore was dangerously *déclassé*. Aretha is, after all, a preacher's daughter. Would Lena Horne play to a mob of unwashed teenagers sitting on the floor? Moreover, Bill Graham could not pay the twenty thousand dollars a show which Ruth Bowen demands on Aretha's behalf. But Aretha was becoming impatient with such high-tone stuffiness. Once Mrs. Bowen was assured the money (Atlantic agreed to underwrite the three days by making a record of it), she went along.

Jerry Wexler got a solid plug inserted in *Rolling Stone* to put the word out (San Francisco would be blown into the Bay, Wexler promised), and the three nights sold out immediately.

Music results from taking enjoyment in the creation of sound. It requires discipline and patience, but no self-denial. When I was in school, music meant playing from books, years of study, memorization, and cruelly hard work. Even after all that you could never be as great as people who had been dead for centuries. An aura of reverence surrounded the gods of classical music. One was not supposed to put false gods before them. Now, when the beauty of "classical music" is opening to me more, I feel it was not that music but an incomprehension of all music which created that repellent aura.

Sensing a fear of human equality in the exaggerated respect for a "bunch of dead Germans," I was attracted to the "everybody welcome" feeling of black American music. Since I first heard the Benny Goodman Carnegie Hall record and began to respond to music with enthusiasm, black music has been a beacon and inspiration. What I hear in it I want to hear more of.

The growth of black American music has been synonymous with the growth of a consciousness. Wedded to electricity, the music has communicated that consciousness with a contagious excitement. The idea it expresses has emerged in the classic way new ideas, like Protestantism, emerge. Everybody, both for and against, knows what this idea is. The idea of black American music is:

> *BOOGIE*
> *BOOGIE*
> *BOOGIE*
> *BOOGIE*
> *BOOGIE 'TIL YOU'RE DONE*
> *BOOGIE*
> *BOOGIE*
> *BOOGIE*
> *BOOGIE*
> *BOOGIE 'CAUSE IT'S FUN*
> *BOOGIE MEAT*
> *BOOGIE SOUL*
> *BOOGIE NOW*
> *AN' THEN SOME MO'*

Jerry Wexler, his pajamas royal blue, was in bed with the flu at the Huntington Hotel, San Francisco's equivalent of New York's Carlyle (Aretha was at the rather more brassy Fairmont across California Street). It was a pleasure to meet him, for Wexler, executive vice-president of Atlantic, is indisputably one of the powers of the black music industry and has been for nearly twenty years. As right-hand man for Ahmet and Nesui Ertegun, who owned the company until they sold it to the Kinney-Warner conglomerate in 1969, he helped make Atlantic the most important of the R&B-jazz independent record companies.

The "indies" had always competed fiercely among themselves. They also fought an often losing battle against the "majors"—the downtown record companies—whose money, prestige, and power could lure away the most successful talent painstakingly developed by the little companies.

Only the fit survived; Atlantic flourished. While most of the indies were run by scrappy businessmen whose horizons were only a bit wider than those of the black artists they had under contract, the Erteguns and Wexler were at home both in the rough-and-tumble indy world and in the drawing rooms of the rich and polite. Mongo Santamaria plays at Ertegun parties which are photographed for *Vogue,* and Wexler can growl "listen, motherfucker" to a dj on one line as he keeps a countess on hold. Likewise in sound: the "Atlantic style" melds unquestionable funk with sophistication and flawless musicality. "We like a little *bel canto* on our stuff," says Wexler. The company has had its share of unexciting talent, but all its products are finely crafted.

Atlantic has had more than its share of exciting talent. The company officially designates Ray and Aretha as its two "geniuses" (though Aretha has not had a "genius" LP), but it has also had John Coltrane and the MJQ. Atlantic brought Otis Redding and the whole Stax-Volt roster from Memphis to international attention, and since the mid-1960s has scored spectacularly

with its first forays into white pop-rock. Eric Clapton may some-day be a "genius," and Iron Butterfly, Led Zeppelin, and Crosby, Stills, Nash, and Young have been among the biggest earners in the post-1967 music boom. The key to success in the record business, says Ralph Bass, is "finding the bodies"—recog-nizing talent, getting it signed and in the studio. Atlantic has this key, plus salesmanship. The company pushes its product with a determination so dogged that it must spring from devo-tion. Wexler is a businessman but "with a heart for the music." The label is known as a good label; musicians and listeners tend to trust Atlantic as a company that keeps its side of the bargain.

Wexler shook hands and brought out a joint. His face was friendly, greyly leonine, his voice gruff. A one-time journalist (at *Billboard*) and still a would-be writer, he likes to talk to report-ers. Today there were three at his bedside. He spoke of the weekend ("We want these longhairs to *listen* to this lady; after that there'll be no problems"), of why the Erteguns and he had sold Atlantic to the Kinney Corporation ("It comes down to, unless you sell, you can't realize what you worked your life to get in a form you can pass on, like to your kids"), and said that we shouldn't be talking to him but to Art Rupe of Specialty Records or Al Bihari of Modern ("They were the cats who did the hard work to get the music out of the ghetto. It wasn't the big companies that were hip to black music, man, it was the indies. Dedicated guys like Georgie Goldner, he found Frankie Lyman, dig?"). He said the American music-buying public is still racially prejudiced, consistently preferring white imitations to the real thing. "You can sell black stuff now, sure, but you gotta fight for it."

Wexler's combination of cynicism and nostalgia, anecdote and innuendo, was captivating—we were getting the straight dope from the man who knew. His charm is famous; one reason for Atlantic's high critical esteem is that there are few music writers who do not consider it an honor to know Jerry Wexler.

My intentions were specific: I wanted to find out why Ray

Charles had left Atlantic for ABC-Paramount at the end of the 1950s. That event has divided Ray's career in half, and though his post-Atlantic years and output double those of his time with Atlantic, many still consider the move a self-crippling mistake. The standard explanation is that Ray left for money; the standard implication is that Ray sold out.

At Atlantic Ray had grown from a blues pianist-singer to a master and synthesizer of all known black music idioms; in his decade-plus at ABC he has added every white idiom to his bag, making hits with country and western tunes, pop standards, and modern rock 'n' roll. Today he is an idiom unto himself, creative beyond the reach of comparative or categorical evaluation—"the only genius in our business," according to Frank Sinatra. His powers of musical invention and emotional expression appear limitless.

His new music (which includes a breath-taking version of "Indian Love Call"), however, is by some taken less seriously than the "legendary" Atlantic sides made "before he added all those strings." Purists, led by Jerry Wexler, persist in vain hopes for "the old Ray" to return. "I say nobody can beat Ray on stage," he said that afternoon. "It's just that he hasn't made a good record in years."

In the liner notes of *The Ray Charles Story,* Volumes One and Two, an Atlantic "greatest hits" repackaging job released after Charles left Atlantic, Wexler spelled out the purist canon. In November, 1954, Ray was "full fledged . . . nothing basic has been added since that day, just more of the same," Wexler wrote. In 1959, after two years of "reluctance," Charles was dubbed "genius," and an album featuring strings and a large band was released. Wexler does not mention that shortly thereafter Ray signed with ABC. He does say that "listeners who weren't quite ready for the unvarnished Charles brand of musical truth found the strings-and-voices palatable." Ray had, however, *really* "changed not one iota" from the small R&B combo days. Wexler finishes by commenting that Ray has not been

writing many songs of late and that "in some listening segments, there is a marked preference for the early, seven-piece,
hard-hitting gospel style."

Why did Ray Charles leave Atlantic? I did not find out, for
Jerry Wexler, the man at Atlantic who most closely handled
Ray's recording career, said he did not know. He had, he said,
"followed Ray all around the country with a contract in my
hand," but to no avail. Why? "For one thing, as you know, Ray
is blind, so he has *aides*, dig, and for them the status quo means
nothing's happening. They like change. So they got Ray's ear—
maybe they inflamed suspicions in his mind, who knows—but
they were saying 'go for money.' Maybe it was that he wanted
to be on a major label, to 'make it,' get away from the indy
background." Was there any conflict between himself and Ray,
any bad feeling? "No, absolutely *none*. Ray and I have *never*
fallen out personally."

The conversation drifted on. Wexler spoke of Aretha's drinking ("though she's got it under control now, I think"), added
that he'd speak to her about giving interviews, but that maybe
she'd be difficult, and then started hyping Donny Hathaway, a
young black singer who might be "another Ray." If we came
back the next day we could hear a dub of his new record. He
was full of praise for the late King Curtis, who after years as a
regular Atlantic studio man was being groomed as a producer.
Curtis, said Wexler, "has a sense of organization, of getting
things done sensibly," and the company had high hopes for him.
"He's not your standard big-name artist who's a hopeless ego-
centric about how important he is." I asked him what and who
he might mean. Wexler looked surprised, as if to say, doesn't
everybody know that artists are basically egotistical? "I'm not
naming names," he said, "that's a whole can of worms I won't
open."

I did not interview Aretha Franklin that weekend. Not that
I was refused; the three times we spoke Aretha was polite. The
second and third times she pointedly remembered my name.
The interview didn't happen because at heart I did not want to

sit, pad in hand, asking her questions. A reporter for ten years, I have been interviewing musicians for seven, drawn to them by an uncontrollable love of their music. My reporter's mask got me closer to them than the average fan in the street could get, yet it left me stuck in a frustrating "role." I seldom felt I could be myself with those whom I queried and wrote about. The awkwardness of it all seemed to contradict the spirit of the music.

A few months before that weekend I had picked up the guitar myself, and from this new vantage point of musicianship, however lowly, I had less desire to ask Aretha about influences and plans. Her music was what she was saying that weekend. I wanted to listen, not question. It was a disappointment not to interview her, but there were compensations. When I told Cornell Dupree, who had been playing guitar with King Curtis for twelve years, that I knew three chords, he said, "Blessings upon you," and shook my hand.

Cornell Dupree plays guitar like an angel. Gangly and boyish, he's got a big grin and long fingers. All weekend I seldom saw him off the stage: he was the first to start playing, the last to stop —except perhaps for Jerry Jermott on bass, who is taller and more sombre. King Curtis, as bandleader, was often in conference with arranger Arif Mardin or Bill Graham, but he too was playing every available minute. So was drummer Bernard Purdie, when he wasn't talking with pretty girls. King Curtis and the Kingpins were men ready to make music at a moment's notice, falling into it as smoothly as sleep. They smiled a lot, particularly organist Billy Preston, never showed bad temper, and got along together with a male camaraderie that was sure and relaxed. This was a gig and a good one. They worked it the best they knew, but the work was play, and they could whistle on the job.

*Ahmet Ertegun announced this week on behalf of Kinney Services Inc. that Kinney has obtained world-wide rights to recordings by the Rolling Stones. . . . These records will be released world-wide on a newly created label called Rolling Stones Rec-*

*ords... [and] will be distributed by Atco Records, of the Atlantic-Atco-Cotillion group in the United States and by Warner Bros. in Canada. . . .*

*Marshall Chess, on behalf of Kinney, will coordinate the activities of the new label and will handle liaison among all of the companies involved.*

*Mr. Ertegun said 'It is one of the most important moments in the history of the Kinney group (which includes the Atlantic, Warner Bros./Reprise and Elektra companies) to be associated with this most outstanding rock and roll band.'*

Kinney news release, April, 1971

Back in the 1940s, when the WASPs still believed in their divine right to rule America, movies were the national entertainment as surely as baseball was the national sport. Vaudeville was dead, Broadway had begun its decline, and the nightclubs and dance halls were not doing the massive business they had done before and during the Depression. "Hollywood" was a byword the world over; at home and abroad, movies commanded the big money, the big audiences, and the big talent. The most American art, it was also a most American business. The major studios, by controlling their own theaters and distribution networks, divided the bulk of the take among themselves, just as the giants of "Detroit" controlled the profits of the national vehicle.

Movies no longer hold that position. Television robbed them of their automatic audience, and the studio system broke down. Films could be made cheaper in London and Rome; Los Angeles became one film capital among many. Although much of "Hollywood" is now making television shows, it is not the once-dreaded TV which is taking the silver screen's place at the top of America's entertainment pyramid—it is popular music.

In the 1960s the recorded-music industry experienced a growth of business and profits which staggered its own imagination. "We've become a billion-dollar industry," Jerry Wexler says often and incredulously; one hears the same self-reminder intoned by other record execs. The trade has been able to sell more and more records at higher and higher prices, complete the switch to stereo and start on quadraphonic, and simultaneously push taped music in reel-to-reel, cartridge, and cassette form, as well as marketing ever more exotic player systems and new paraphernalia like headphones. A new broadcast outlet— FM stereo—is now airing the record industry's products in a velvet-gloved version of the high-pressure AM sell, and a whole field of journalism has been created to review, generally glorify, and publicize records. Records were once sold from behind counters in small record stores; now they are stacked six feet high beside ringing registers in discount sound supermarkets.

The billion-dollar turning point came in 1967. Until then the 45 disc was the most important medium for rock 'n' roll; LPs were still associated more with musics that sold to smaller markets. But in the 1960s, just as books in paper had found their way out of the bookstores and into the drugstores, LPs got onto "the racks"—the trade's name for all non-record-store sales outlets—at supermarkets, discount centers, and at department stores in the new shopping plazas. *Sgt. Pepper* was crucial. For three years the Beatles had been on top, but their market, although bigger than any rock market before them, was still primarily the teen 45-disc market. The new wave of interest in rock generated by San Francisco and psychedelia was the first real challenge to the Beatles and the British movement. Would the Beatles sink or swim? They triumphed with a masterpiece that lent all of their prestige to psychedelic and electronic music, summed it up, and then transcended it. Their record established the "album" as the new expressive unit for rock 'n' roll, and joined the rock market to the pop market to create a new "youth" market, the upper limit of which was now thirty-five, not nineteen. Since then, 45 sales have declined relative to album sales, and rock-pop figures like Carole King are selling to an audience so diverse as to be virtually uncategorizable.

By riding all of that Kinney, with its parking-lot origins, is now in an aesthetic-economic relationship to its time not unlike that of a major film studio in the 1930s and 1940s. Kinney makes money from the Stones, Aretha, the late Jimi Hendrix and Otis

Redding and Jim Morrison, Eric Clapton, Woodstock (records, film, and name on T-shirts, kites, etc.), Little Richard, Steve Stills, the Grateful Dead, Judy Collins, Paul Butterfield, Roberta Flack, Randy Newman, the Incredible String Band, Wilson Pickett, Alice Cooper, Dr. John the Night Tripper, and many, many more. Only Columbia is as big, and Columbia, the very model of a modern major "major," is big: Santana, Bob Dylan, Barbra Streisand, Johnny Cash, Johnny Mathis, Taj Mahal, Earl Scruggs, and Miles Davis. All these stars are horses in the conglomerate stables. Records by the stars, or by combinations of the stars, are like the MGM and Warner Brothers films of thirty years ago: they can be seen as the shifting collaborations of artists under studio contracts. The Joe Cocker-Leon Russell LPs are like the musical comedies which featured one or two stars against a foil of familiar faces. Mick Jagger has compared his life to Cary Grant's.

The history of the movie-to-music evolution is complex, but Kinney's growth suggests it well. Warner Brothers entered the 1960s as a great studio, yet not the power it had been. Frank Sinatra, a pop star who had to go to Hollywood to make it *really* big, made it even bigger by starting Reprise Records. Its success attracted Warners, which was looking for new entertainment resources to offset the insecurity of movie profits. Warners bought Reprise. Then in a David-Goliath deal typical of 1960s financing, little Seven Arts, a film production company, bought Warners/Reprise. The next series of purchases happened so fast that even company employees were unsure of who was selling what to whom. In the end, Warners added Atlantic to itself in a deal that gave Atlantic's Ahmet Ertegun more power than the head music man at Warners. Another series of moves brought in Ted Ashley from the Ashley Famous Agency (which became Marvin Josephson's International Famous Agency) to reign as entertainment tycoon for the whole of Kinney, which bought Warners and Atlantic. This show-biz empire-building was so earthshakingly immense that its tremors reached even me—my agent, who was with Josephson, moved a few blocks to the IFA offices, and her stationery changed.

Barely had all that settled when I heard that Kinney had also bought Elektra, rounding out its consolidation of the independents. The companies remained distinct labels, but their distribution systems and many internal company services were pooled. The addition of Marshall Chess to their executive roster was the final and perfect ironic touch: Marshall is the beloved son of the late Leonard Chess, founder of Chess Records, the prototypical ghetto independent and home of the Chicago blues upon which the Rolling Stones based their music. Meanwhile Chess Records was bought by the GRT Corporation, a tape conglomerate, and its offices moved from Chicago's South Side to Manhattan. The one-time majors—Decca, Capitol, and RCA Victor—have continued with catalogues little changed since Eddie Fisher and "How Much Is That Doggie in the Window," the point when, borne by the indies, black American music entered the white popular market.

> *Yeah,*
> *She's 36 in the bust*
> *28 in the waist*
> *44 in the hips*
> *She got real crazy legs . . .*
>
> *She's not too tall*
> *Complexion is fair*
> *Man, she knocks me out*
> *The way she wears her hair*
>
> *You upset me baby*
> *You upset me, baby*
> *Like being hit by a falling tree,*
> *Baby, what you do to me!**

*"You Upset Me Baby" by Jules Taub and Riley B. King. © 1954 Modern Music Publishing Company and Sounds of Lucille Publishing Company. Used by permission. All rights reserved.

Aretha Franklin is short and round. Her clothes—high boots, short knit dresses, sunglasses, and costume jewelry—are stylish and expensive, but, though they suit her, they are not glamorous. She is a lovely black sister, not a willowy show-biz singer like Diana Ross or Dionne Warwick, whose well-earned successes have in part depended on their stunning faces and figures. Aretha's beauty, while no less apparent than theirs, is more internal. At rehearsals her movements were restrained, her demeanor quiet. The Sweethearts of Soul, her back-up singers, with curly wigs and patent leather bags, flirted and carried on like schoolgirls; Aretha stayed in the background when she wasn't singing. Her eyes took everything in but gave little back.

She was, of course, working hard, preparing not only for three shows in an unfamiliar and challenging milieu, but also to make a record—which, in her art, is the medium of permanent statement. Yet how much was it *her* record? It would be called an Aretha Franklin record, and all depended on her, but all was not directed by her. Producer Wexler, Bill Graham, King Curtis, arranger Arif Mardin, and Ruth Bowen were, however subtly, more in charge than she. They deferred to her every spoken wish; when she did not speak, they decided.

The tension between Aretha as a Negro woman singer and Aretha as an adventurous artist in the popular music medium, was palpable. She was not making her record the way her white male contemporaries, Bob Dylan, John Lennon, the Stones, or Leon Russell make theirs—on their own with friends, delivered as tapes to submissive corporations. On the other hand she was far freer than in her days at Columbia or when she was Atlantic's brand new success in 1967. Here she was this weekend, the ranking black singer of the day, playing the Fillmore—in much the same position, four crucial years on, as Otis Redding had been at the Monterey Pop Festival in 1967. Where might Otis' music have gone after "Dock of the Bay," written on a Sausalito houseboat during a Fillmore engagement? The Fillmore audience had certainly changed B. B. King's music and career—how would it change hers? Might it help her break the constrictions of race and sex that still webbed her in?

Her quietness that weekend suggested determination. As photographers came close to snap and snap at her again, she looked deeply into their lenses and did not smile. Wexler kissed her on the cheek when he arrived on stage Friday afternoon; Aretha was unmoved. When no one could figure out the words of Steve Stills' "Love the One You're With," Aretha listened to all suggestions, then said she'd sing it the way it made sense to *her*. Her short natural hair revealed a strong neck.

She was smoking, not chain smoking but almost, menthol cigarette after menthol cigarette. Blues singers have never tried to save their voices—the idea would be nearly incomprehensible to them—and Aretha is a blues singer. Yet an opera singer with Aretha's voice would take care of her throat as a delicate and irreplaceable musical instrument deserves to be taken care of. I found myself wishing that Aretha would stop smoking. Her cigarettes seemed part of her guard; why should she turn the tensions of her struggle against herself?

Black American music has had many names. Blues, boogie-woogie, jazz, R&B, rock 'n' roll, soul, gospel, work songs, swing, funk, bop, be-bop, the Mashed Potatoes, the Swim, the Jerk, the Fly, the Twist. "Music that is inspiring to the head *and* heart, to dance by and cause you to pat your foot," says Chuck Berry.

Recently I visited a class at Berkeley. A group of black kids dominated the hour-and-a-half lecture and scared everybody. One kid was almost as good as Little Richard, fast and piercing, hurling questions and slashing the air with a pointed finger. The kids said they were not hostile, "just trying to find out what the fuck is actually happening, man." Anger did spill out of one of them; he screamed "motherfucker" and "asshole" a lot. I got scared and annoyed, telling myself, "Arrogant bastards, hung-up black cats," but I found that if I listened to their words—which was all that was happening, harmless old words—I agreed with everything they said.

I decided to get close to them, walked up to where they sat, and sat down. I was nervous and said how frightened I had been even though I dug them. The Little Richard guy first waved me away; he preferred to talk to five hundred people. I said, "You seem tense." He said, "You'd be tense if you were me." "I can dig it," I said. "Boy, am I tense, I am fucked *up!*" Somewhere in there I realized that *he* did not scare me, I was scared already.

Friday night went off well. Tower of Power was exuberant and earnest, and nearly dwarfed by what followed them. But they were part of the Bill Graham–Fillmore empire, and the weekend was good promotional exposure. King Curtis and the Kingpins were a knockout, Aretha superb. The song order got mixed up at one point, King Curtis calling one tune when Aretha wanted another. Aretha did Curtis' song and seemed mildly miffed, but it was just a first-night rough spot, and the crowd went home satisfied.

Saturday afternoon I went back to the Huntington to hear the new Donny Hathaway LP which Wexler had hyped to the skies. Again a group of writers, out came the joints, on went the record. Otherwise a respectful silence. I found myself not liking the record, pulled out my notebook, and wrote: "Jerry Wexler is saying this guy is a fit and possible inheritor of the mantle of Ray and Aretha. I hear him as a supertalented musician, backed by brilliant instrumentalists, but an unsure young man, inclined to sentimentality and to a little-boy appeal which lacks the manliness that Ray had at nineteen and the pride and striving for freedom that characterizes every note that Aretha ever sung."

As he flipped the record, Wexler said, "He's conservatory trained." That I could hear, but little else. If this was Wexler's third genius, Hathaway sounded like his first false genius. Genius one had gone to another label, genius two was asserting herself; was Hathaway a genius who would stay *Wexler's* genius? The record ended.

Wexler said he had a tape of *Young, Gifted, and Black*, Aretha's latest work in progress. It was still a rough mix, and most of the horn and string tracks had not been added, but he'd play it anyway. It was beautiful. The arrangements she had worked out for the background vocalists were smooth as smoke. Her piano tinkled like Errol Garner and rang with the authority of classical harmonies. "I see a brand new girl," she sang in one song; that's how she sounded. I couldn't just listen and sang along. (When released in 1972, the record exceeded the promise of that afternoon's foretaste.)

As I was leaving, Wexler spoke to me at the door: "You know, I didn't *really* mean it about Donny." Aretha's voice was still coming out from the little tape machine. "Wow," he said, "the music *pours* out of her!"

Saturday night was, well, stupendous. There are many ways for an R&B horn section to play a phrase, but it sounds best if they come in *absolutely* on time and full strength from the first instant, so that there is no ragged fade-up from silence, but a sudden punch of sound. Wayne Jackson's Memphis Horns were as crisp as karate Saturday night. Wayne is small, plays trumpet, runs the Horns as an extremely successful business, and says that "playing music is 99 percent confidence." The group was once known as the Mar-Keys and can be heard on almost every Otis Redding record and on the records of every singer who wants soulful brass and who can afford to hire them—plus many TV commercials. They are all Southern boys; several, including Wayne, are white. For some reason they ended up blowing in Memphis, not picking in Nashville, but it's all music from the same part of the world.

Bernard "Pretty" Purdie is as good-natured as the beat he keeps. The demand for his propulsive drumming has kept him shuttling in taxis between studios, morning to night, for a decade. King Curtis—the master of the stuttering sax. He played ballads with a surprising tenderness and loved to howl uptempo. He was *the* R&B saxophone player, responsible for most of those rocking sax breaks you remember from the fifties, composer of "Soul Serenade," and a New York City session man of the first rank. Curtis was big, at least six feet three inches, with the heavy gut of a muscular man living the life of steaks and import beer. All weekend he wore a black leather jacket with a white leather horse's head coming through a horseshoe on the back. (Curtis, born Curtis Ousley in Fort Worth, Texas, was stabbed to death in New York less than six months after the Fillmore weekend. Witnesses said he was outside on the sidewalk arguing with tenants of a building he owned when one attacked him. Aretha sang and the Kingpins and the Horns played at his funeral, which was attended by everyone in soul music show biz.)

Jackson, Purdie, Curtis—complete musicians. Their idiom is rhythm-and-blues, technically more sophisticated than in its raucous early days in the late forties and early fifties, but with the same funky power. The point of it is to entertain, make 'em dance; there's not much thought about art. Yet the idiom in no way restricts the musicians; they love to play, and play the music they love. It comes out R&B. Fun, for an R&B cat, is to find ways to increase the dramatic contrasts within a song, to create ever more intense rhythms. That's what people like, colorful songs with drive, songs you can get the feel of and feel with.

Curtis and company came on stage Saturday night and started out with "Knock on Wood," a Stax-Volt classic. They sounded the way they looked: the trumpets gleaming in the stage lights, Purdie rocketing away, his eyes seldom leaving Curtis' swaying back, Jermott's fingers bounding up and down the long black neck of his bass, Dupree light and pretty on guitar. After three bars you realized what fun it was to be there, one of those paradises everyone hopes will dot their lives. (Atlantic has released *King Curtis at Fillmore West*, recorded that weekend. It is as powerful as Aretha's record.)

It was pleasant to be in the crowd that night. The grass roots that Aretha drew were not hippies but black teenagers, most of them, like Aretha, in the Fillmore for the first time. They were kids like none I ever knew—Afros, self-assured, smoking grass and drinking wine. Some were overdressed for sitting on the floor (I saw guys worrying about the crease in their slacks), but they weren't Negroes, but something new.

Aretha herself was in a trailer parked outside the stage door. A waiter from one of San Francisco's better restaurants took in a meal on a silver tray. She was the star, and when she came on stage she earned her position all over again. There were no rough spots Saturday night. Sometime I scribbled in my notebook, "Billy Preston—INSPIRED!"

I took a rough poll of the musicians that weekend on how they were betting the Ali-Frazier fight. Without exception they were betting on Ali. The Kingpins were to play at his post-fight party. About half called him Muhammad Ali, the other half said Cassius Clay.

The great ship of Western music has in the past twenty years drastically altered its course. Chuck Berry saw which way it was headed, for it was Berry and his friends who had slipped up out of steerage and seized the helm.

Aretha and Ray sat together at the Sunday-night dinner party before the show. Their table was right beside the line waiting for ribs and greens. It was as much a receiving line as a food line. They both shook dozens of hands, and everyone with an Instamatic got a snap. They didn't appear to talk much; they hardly could have in the circumstances. When not being spoken to, Ray was quiet, even withdrawn. Wexler waved me over to shake hands with him. Introducing me, he told Ray I was writing an article and was "into your music." "I'm glad of *that*," Ray replied, meaning the latter.

In 1971, Ralph J. Gleason, who has been following the growth of black American music for thirty years, wrote a reflective column on the mysterious and virtually unpublicized death of Albert Ayler, a jazz musician whose body was found in New York's East River. The low significance the American public accorded Ayler's death angered Gleason. As if in defiance, he made the strongest prediction of his career: that soon, in the near future, there would be a "coming together of all musics." What could he mean? Wouldn't it be something!

Sunday night—I've already described that. Listening to the record now, I can hear what happened as I did not hear it then —we were too busy making it happen. I remember that when Aretha shouted something about, "Every now and then you gotta sit down, cross your legs, cross your arms, and say, 'Yes, Lord,'" I had an image of a middle-aged black lady like Rosa Parks on that bus in Montgomery, Alabama, or maybe Beulah, and I figured that feeling like them would feel fine.

Aretha, in white and gold, was so beautiful that night, her voice soaring, her energy awesome. "You have been more to me than anything I could ever have expected," she called out toward the end. "You too, you too," we tried to tell her back. She came down the runway. Hands reached up to touch her, she reached down to touch them. When it was over, it felt like a new beginning.

If Ali had won the next night, you could have convinced me we were about to enter the promised land.

Georgia, Oh-h-h-h Georgia,

No peace I find,

Just an old sweet song . . .*

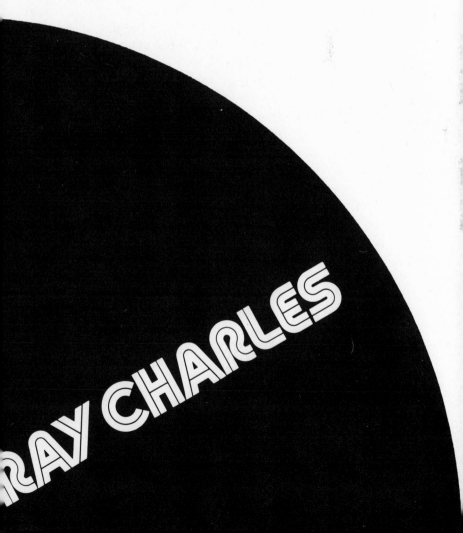

RAY CHARLES

● Ray Charles, bathed in light, sweat gleaming on his brow, sang "Georgia on My Mind." The song, written by Hoagy Carmichael and Stuart Gorrell in 1930, was a huge hit for him in 1960 and has since become one of his classics. Ray Charles has no one theme song; he has made two or perhaps three dozen songs *his* in his career of nearly three decades. A few bars of any of them are a signature recognized with pleasure by millions around the world. "Georgia" holds a unique place in his heart and in the hearts of his fans. Twelve years after the hit, he still sings it at most shows. Opening night, a Tuesday, at the Circle Star Theater, November, 1972, was one of them. His rendering of the song has changed little over the years. The strings which frame his voice so lushly on record are absent in concert, but muted horns play the same role. The tempo is still slow. His blue passion has been tempered by countless remeditations on the theme; the moonlight through the pines is ever more evocative and ethereal.

In his present arrangement, when he gets to the repeat of "Other arms reach out to me," he plays softly on piano. The band is silent except for bass and brushed drums. As he holds the note on "arms," however, he wants a flute to echo his phrase, and to do the same thing as he holds the "me"; likewise at the middle and end of the next line, "Other *eyes* smile tenderly." When he came to that point Tuesday night, tenor saxophonist Andy Ennis, doubling as usual on flute, began to play just as Ray got to "arms"—immediately Ray's head swiveled from his mike and faced down into the band's lower half of the stage. "You came in too early," he said in a shout-whisper—"reach out to me," he sang. Ennis played it that way again. Again Ray's head turned: "Andy, you're coming in too damn early." Ray was pissed. The next line went right. When he closed the song, Ray's irritation was gone, but he said again and firmly for the record, "You were starting too early, man." The next night they didn't play "Georgia"; the night after that they did, and it was fine.

The Circle Star stands surrounded by its own parking lot

beside the Bayshore Freeway in San Carlos, California, thirty miles down the suburban Peninsula from San Francisco. A theater in the round with a revolving stage, it has done well and badly in cycles, and the present owners, Marquee Productions (Sammy Davis Jr. is a principal stockholder), are the third group to manage it. The theater now hopes to fill its thirty-five hundred seats by offering, at home and at reasonable prices ($7.50 top), the same talent that headlines at Tahoe, Reno, and Las Vegas. Only dependable draws like Jack Benny, however, pull in enough middle-aged and prosperous suburbanites to show a profit. Otherwise the theater does best with acts that get out kids and blacks *and* the suburbanites: Woody Allen, Ella Fitzgerald and Count Basie, Pearl Bailey, Bill Withers and Lily Tomlin, the Supremes. The sound and lighting are good; once adjusted to, the slow circling of the stage is magical. The decor is a neutral tan and green with an emphasis on durability (the walls are undisguised cinderblock); wallpaper and a red carpet in the lobby give the necessary hint of elegance. A grillroom restaurant, a cocktail lounge, and champagne and snack bars serve the dressed-up crowds, out for a special night on the town.

The Ray Charles Show was at the Circle Star for six days, one show nightly Tuesday through Friday, two on Saturday night, and a Sunday matinee and evening show. The entertainment featured Ray, his band (sometimes called the Leroy Cooper Orchestra), the Raelets, and ventriloquist-comedian Aaron Williams and his dummy, Freddy. B. B. King, a "special guest attraction," opened each show; after intermission Ray's band came on to do "Our Suite," a rambling but effective overture. The Raelets joined them for a few numbers, then went off to make way for Aaron and Freddy. When he had gotten a struggling Freddy back into his suitcase, Aaron split. Charles was announced ("the Geen-yus, 1972"), and on he came, led down the aisle and up the ramp by his valet Bob Taylor.

Waves of applause, whoops of primed and expectant delight, greeted Ray every night. His left arm was linked with Taylor's, his right he held high in salute. Taylor took him to the corner of the Fender Rhodes electric piano; its keyboard made an ell with that of the Yamaha grand. Once Ray had touched the Fender, he knew where he was, and Taylor walked away. Ray then saluted the audience with both arms, a big smile on his face. Slowly and with several pauses to indicate that he was attempting to take the whole crowd into his embrace, he wrapped both arms tight around his body, bent low, rose, then loosed his arms to wave again, ebulliently this time. Only then did the cheering begin to fade, and using his right hand to guide himself, he reached the padded-leather piano stool and sat down.

The band's fanfare of greeting matched the crowd's and diminished with it; though bass and drums kept up a pulse, Ray played his first chords to silence. His fingers hit the keys with bounce, a growl that ended in a yelp sprang from his throat, and his feet started a dance that did not stop for an hour and a half; although at times his movements grew so wild that his crashing onto the floor seemed imminent, that never happened. He played against the beat; the band clapped in unison on it. Clap clap. Three quick bluesy chords. Clap clap. A sudden run in the right hand over heavy explorations by the left. Clap clap. When he felt settled on stage and in touch with the band, he waved the warm-up groove to a close, setting off instantly into a fast-paced "Marie" ("the dawn is breaking"). "Marie," written by Irving Berlin (a hit for, among others, Frank Sinatra with Tommy Dorsey in 1940), is almost as familiar as a folk song; it maintains a quaint gentility and is seldom played today except as a nostalgia piece. Ray's version was rippingly immediate, and as he closed he adlibbed a shouted string of "Marie, Marie, Mar*ie*, oh Marie don't you *know*" over the band's blaring finale.

Then "Georgia." Charles again waited for a hush, let a chord ring softly, then spoke. "Every time I sing this song . . ." A pause and a new, more oblique chord. "It reminds me of . . ." A longer pause. His hands fell to his side: "My . . ." And then the song began.

When he was still a child, Ray Charles has said many times, he knew he had to do *something;* otherwise the future would be a cup, a cane, and a box of pencils. His realism was precocious but necessary, and has stood him in good stead for forty-three years. He was born September 23, 1930 in Albany, Georgia. His parents, Bailey and Areatha Robinson, moved south across the state line to Greenville, Florida, about the end of that year. They were poor. Bailey Robinson worked for the railroad and did all kinds of handy work; he was, Ray has said, "a man of his word," respected by all who knew him, white and black. Areatha Robinson stacked planks in Greenville's sawmill and cooked and washed for the white families in the tiny town. Ray dropped the "Robinson" when he started playing on his own to avoid confusion with the great light-heavyweight boxer, Sugar Ray Robinson, but to him, if to few others, it is still his last name. Several of his recent LPs list Ray Robinson as the engineer.

When Ray was five his baby brother George fell into a full washtub in the back yard. Ray tried to pull him out but could not. He ran for his mother; when she came the baby had already drowned. Shortly thereafter thick mucouslike tears started to leak from Ray's eyes. A painful pressure built up behind them, and over many months his vision grew less distinct. Medical help in the rural Depression-wracked South was a financial and practical impossibility. By seven Ray was stone-blind.

Areatha Robinson refused to let her son be crippled by his handicap. She kept him at chores and let him bang into tables and chairs until he learned his way about. When he started school at the state's St. Augustine School for Deaf and Blind Children in Orlando, his mother had already taught him to print his ABCs, and he had made his piano debut at the cafe of a Mr. Wiley Pittman. Mr. Pittman played boogie-woogie piano and let five-year-old R. C. tinkle away on the high keys. One day when he had a few friends there, he asked Ray to play on his own. "And if I didn't have the nerve to go and get shy," he has said. "But I sat there moving my left hand back and forth and banging with my right. The people clapped to make me feel good. From that point on I loved to play music."

In Orlando he studied classical piano and played jazz on the side, experimented with alto sax and clarinet, and learned enough theory to make up and dictate band arrangements. When Ray was fifteen, Areatha Robinson died of food poisoning —a bad sweet-potato pie. Her husband passed away soon after, and Ray was alone as his mother had often said he would be one day. He took a room with friends of his parents in Jacksonville and got himself jobs playing piano at parties and on local radio. Despite some gigs with swing bands in Jacksonville and Orlando, he almost starved until he hooked up with a white hillbilly group, the Florida Playboys. On Pittman's juke box he had heard all the black blues then on record; with the Playboys he learned to yodel the white blues he had loved on WSM's Grand Ole Opry broadcast from Nashville. When he had six hundred dollars saved up ("My only interest was music and getting my hands on some money," he told Whitney Balliet), he took a bus to the one city that wasn't too big and scary but was as far from the South as he could get and still be in the USA: Seattle.

Ray got off the bus, slept twenty-four hours, woke at two in the morning, found an after-hours club called the Rocking Chair, pleaded his way in, sang "Driftin' Blues," and knocked 'em dead. He organized a trio of piano, bass, and electric guitar and started working all the clubs in town. "He was R. C. to us," remembers Quincy Jones. "When we first met I was fourteen, he was sixteen. But he seemed to me like thirty-two. He always knew exactly what to do. It was like a clan, the musicians in Seattle then. Groups were tight. It was the age of jamming; Ray would finish up his four gigs for the night and hurry over to the Elks or the Black and Tan. The gigs were bread and butter. It was that jamming that mattered." These talented young men played the jazzy cool-hot blues which was all the rage. They devoured every new Charles Brown, Percy Mayfield, and Nat "King" Cole record, learned the latest licks, and proudly laid down their own.

Ray's trio got on local TV, and by 1949 Ray took them down

to Los Angeles to record for Swingtime, an indie. Everest Records, in their Archive of Folk and Jazz Music series, has collected an LP of these sides. The trio cooks, and Ray's voice is remarkably like it is today. He took fewer chances and occasionally seems imitative, but the supple relaxation of phrasing and intonation and the interplay of humor and conviction are all there. At nineteen he sounded like a grown man. For one session he was able to get a band together—trumpet, four saxes, guitar, bass, and drums. Singing against the bigger sound, he had to shout, losing the cool he could keep in the trio setting. "My body is made of heartaches, blues is my middle name," he cries in "Someday." "We used those big transcription discs then," Ray remembers. "That was a long time ago."

In 1950 indies like Swingtime were making LA an important recording center for R&B and jazz (this was also Ralph Bass's West Coast heyday), and though none of his records hit big, Ray moved down to the action from Seattle. He got a spot as an opening attraction on Lowell Fulsom's road show and toured with him all over the Southwest for more than a year. A Texas connection got Fulsom signed up with New York agent Billy Shaw; when Shaw got the show booked at the Apollo, he heard Ray, signed him on his own, and sent him out as a single. Alone except for a brief period leading a group that backed singer Ruth Brown, Ray traveled for three years all across the country, taking what sidemen he could get when he arrived at a gig. It was easier to get jobs working alone, but musically it was risky and frustrating. After a particularly miserable experience in Philadelphia ("that band couldn't read and they couldn't hear either"), he decided he had to have his own band. From the many good musicians he had worked with, he put together a seven-man group in Dallas, borrowed money for a car and station wagon, and went on the road in 1954 as Ray Charles and his Band.

During those years alone, however, he had molded his own style and built up a small following. He had also come to the attention of Atlantic Records, which signed him in 1952. To the company he was then, Jerry Wexler has written, a "journey-man" R&B artist; he sang and played songs and arrangements supplied to him. The results were brilliant; Ray was not a jour-neyman long. In December, 1953, Ray had asked Jerry Wexler and Ahmet Ertegun to record him with a band which he had put together to gig around New Orleans. They cut "Don't You Know," a tune Ray had written, in a radio station. "The side didn't upset the charts," Wexler wrote, but "it was a landmark session in the growth pattern because it had: Ray Charles origi-nals, Ray Charles arrangements, a Ray Charles band. . . . All we could do at the session was see to it that the radio technician didn't erase the good takes during the playbacks."

A year later, after months of rehearsal and steady touring, Ray Charles had his hand-picked Dallas band in Atlanta. Ray called Wexler and Ertegun again. Wexler: "We got with him in the afternoon at the Peacock nightclub, where he had his band set to play for us. Except for Ray and the band, the place was empty, and as soon as we walked in, Ray counted off, and they hit into 'I Got a Woman,' and that was it." They taped that (and "Greenbacks") at a radio station the next day. Like many of the unusual records of that time, "I Got a Woman" was a hybrid: it had the drive of rhythm-and-blues, and the subject matter—a woman "way over town"—was pure blues; the band was jazzy; and the rising feel of the chord progression was like church music. Ray's singing went from spoken voice to shout to falsetto to croon at will, like a preacher's. The blend of idioms made one rocking whole, and the disc sold like hotcakes in the R&B mar-ket and got wide play on the then brand new rock 'n' roll stations. At twenty-four, nine years after he left blind school, Ray Charles had arrived.

"I remember one time we were in Japan, Hiroshima, there were these guys outside my hotel room, in like an alley or vacant lot." Leroy Cooper, a man whose girth ranks with that of the late Mr. Five-by-Five, Jimmy Rushing, stood in a back-stage corridor telling a story to alto sax player Don Garcia.

Garcia, twenty-eight, from Houston, Texas, had been with Ray's band since the previous spring—seven months. A graduate of Boston's Berklee School of Music, he had played in jazz groups around the Hub for years. In LA last spring a friend told him about the April audition and recommended him. "No, auditioning didn't make me nervous," he said. "I knew what I'd have to do in a band like this, and I knew I could do it. I was ready." He was hired, $305 a week starting pay. Cooper, on the other hand, has been with Charles since the first Dallas days. He is the band leader, "musical director" officially; as he spoke, his huge baritone sax rested on top of an aluminum laundry cart (neatly stenciled "Ray Charles Organization, Los Angeles, Calif, USA") down the hall.

"They were practicing karate, judo, something like that. First one guy would rush the other, and the second guy would turn around and, flash, kick backwards. Like this." Cooper attempted a demonstration, a Tiparillo clenched between his teeth. His bulk turned slowly, a heavy right leg lifted and performed a gentle slap at the air. "But they were shouting—haargh! haargh! First one guy would kick, then the other. For hours. I watched 'em til I fell asleep watching." Cooper stared straight ahead with a concentrated air, seeing his memory unfold in his mind's eye.

Cooper has been everywhere with Ray Charles, all the foreign capitals and every burg with a club, a theater, or municipal auditorium in the States. His seventeen years with Ray? "It's been a gas," he said. It was that night: his stomach was bothering him, whether it was a hangover or overeating he wasn't sure. The band had been out to the Oakland hills to a party given by the parents of trombonist Steve Turre, who, like Garcia, is a long-haired man in his twenties. Turre, too, had been with the band since April, the month Ray's touring season begins after a winter of rest, taking care of business, and recording. Come April Ray auditions new players for vacant band spots, rehearses new material, brushes up and reconsiders old songs and arrangements. They tour May to December: a few one-nighters, mostly week-long location dates like the Circle Star, and one or two trips to Europe, the Near East, or the Orient. (After the Circle Star the season had only two more weeks: one at the Valley Theater, near LA, one in Israel.) Band members are on two-week notice; whether they give or get notice depends on "how things work out," said drummer John Perrett.

They hadn't worked out for Perrett, another one-season veteran. He had just given his notice and was sore, glumly hinting at a preferential system which had left him out. "I gained a lot musically, got stronger," he said, "but I'm not sorry I'm going." He didn't know what lay ahead; maybe a tour with Tom Jones' band, hopefully studio work in LA. Another new member was ecstatic to be there: apple-cheeked trumpteter Dave Kelly, who had joined the band after going to a concert in Chicago in September. He had seen a vacant seat in the trumpet section, applied, and got the job. He was twenty-four, and except for a few one-nighters with Doc Severinson's band around Illinois, this was his first real job. "I love it all," he said, "traveling, playing, learning from Ray Charles, wow!" Mike Conlon, thirty-one, another trumpeter of a few months' standing in the band said, "This is the best gig I've ever had, but not the best I'll ever have." Conlon, who had a huge Irish "Afro" and squinty lines around his eyes, had toured with Ike and Tina Turner and Johnny Otis and done three years in jail for marijuana. He had also led his own jazz combo and hopes to again. He was nervous when he auditioned. "I lost seven pounds that day, all sweat. This music is great," he said, "but I'd like to be able to express myself more. Here you have to play the music on those charts."

"Ray Charles is a heavy dude," said tenor sax man James Clay, who had been with the band four years. "But we don't forget that this is a gig. We're *working.*"

At the Circle Star, Ray performed in a colorful variety of mod tuxedos, purple velvet jackets, and suits of rusty gold with contrasting stripes on the trousers. The band had two changes: grey business suits and brown business suits, both worn with white shirts and dark ties. A band valet takes care of cleaning them: all stage clothes belong to Ray Charles Enterprises.

As the stage belongs to Ray. He listens closely to every note band members play. What sounds he does not like are not continued. At the Circle Star, Charles occasionally praised a player with an encouraging, "Work it out, son," during a solo and made jokes about the solemn church-deacon manner of organist John Henderson. Several nights he called Henderson by name to come to the Yamaha when he switched to electric piano, and had him sing one song. "He is helping me out," said Henderson, twenty-five years old. He had studied voice at Texas Southern University and was gigging around Houston when, in June, he filled a sudden vacancy at the band's big Hammond. "He's taught me a bit, he's a beautiful man, but he's not giving anything away."

Ray played the Circle Star with a seventeen-piece ensemble: five saxophones (two altos, two tenors, and Cooper's baritone), four trumpets, four trombones, guitar, bass, drums, and organ. As Aaron's smart-ass dummy Freddy pointed out one night, "There's a few *white* faces down in the hole now." White or black, half those faces will be new next year. Ray gets one sound despite turnover with the help of two dependables stationed at either end of the pit. Leroy Cooper is one: he sits at far stage left. He often stands to conduct the band, and he keeps them working. When the trumpets or trombones have no part to play, they are expected to shake tambourines, hit cowbells, rattle maracas, and, with Cooper's lead, to shout or laugh appropriately. At far stage right, Ray's side, sits bassist Edgar Willis. "Edgar Willis, he's been with me since I *been*," Ray said on stage one night, also playing him the ultimate compliment for a bassist: "One thing I like about Edgar is, he *never* hurries."

Edgar Willis is a tall man, slender and still strong at fifty-one. He has a small bald spot at the back of his head and thick, curly black mustachios. Born in Pittsburgh, he started playing bass as a teenager, studied it seriously in the late 1940s, and was playing with Sonny Stitt in Washington, D.C., in 1957, when Ray

*From left to right: B.B. King, Ray Charles, John Hen-
derson, Vernita Moss, Estella Yarbrough, Mabel John,
Susaye Greene, and Dorothy Berry*

heard and hired him. Willis is a calm man, given to understatement. "I am considered the bass player. We all look to Ray for our cues, but I am stationed closest to him, and he passes messages to me. Maybe if he starts an unfamiliar number, I can quickly sketch out to the others what is required. I think Ray can depend on me to do the things he wants." His devotion to Ray is complete. "He's a great musician, one that any musician would want to meet and work with and for. It doesn't seem to matter what kind of music it is, when he sings it, it says something.

"Oftentimes I'm with the fans who like the old songs, 'What'd I Say,' that stuff, but it seems every time we go around the circuit we gain some listeners, lose others. When you have an audience to please, you have to please them. Ray does a good job at that." Willis chuckled. "I remember a girl back in Pittsburgh. She'd always say, 'Oh, I don't like Ray Charles,' then she heard one of the country and western albums. She flipped."

That Tuesday night the stage was drenched in blue light when Ray started "Yesterday." (The song is in Ray's repertory; it was performed once or twice during the week in San Carlos.) He noodled ruminatively on the piano. What tune was he introducing? Perhaps only Willis knew for sure. He stood and looked intently at Ray, putting his left hand in position on the long neck of his Fender electric bass (his first; until four years ago he played a stand-up bass). He waited, looked at the band, then back at Ray. His right hand he held suspended before him. Ray played on, the chords coming closer together, more rumbling. Willis's right hand started a slow descent to the strings. At the instant he plucked, Ray hit the same low note. "*Yesh*-ti-day . . ."

Ray adlibbed the end as well, extending the last "yesterday" into a long a capella oooohing. At some point he would sing a final note, but when? Willis stood again. The band watched him. He thought Ray was closing, his hand started to fall. But no, Ray held a few beats more. The falling hand rose, and Willis scratched his chin with it. Then the end, down fell his hand, and

Charles and Willis finished in unison. The band got the final chord, and in the ambience of muted regret, John Perrett's brushes set his cymbals shimmering.

"Well, Freddy, what did you think of the election?" Aaron Williams asked the question like a straight man to blandness born. He stood before the mike with one foot up on a metal chair; on his knee he balanced a dummy, Freddy. Like Aaron, Freddy was brown skinned, but he wore a shiny two-tone blue zoot suit, and Aaron wore an anonymous tux. Freddy also had a handle in his back, and despite his angry cries of "Turn me loose, turn me loose!" Aaron kept a firm grip on it. With it he could open and close Freddy's mouth and eyes, raise his eyebrows, and swivel his whole head.

"What election?" Freddy shot back. Before Aaron could answer, Freddy had demanded that Aaron fix his legs so his suit wouldn't get creased, asked a lady in the front row what she was looking at ("Ain't you never seen no black dummy before?"), and shown off a huge ring to the whole crowd (Freddy: "That's my wedding ring"; Aaron: "It's on the wrong hand"; Freddy: "I married the wrong woman"). Aaron tapped Freddy on the shoulder to get his attention. "Don't hit me, man, don't hit me. I'll get so mad I'll chase you down the street so fast you'll have to put your fingers in your nose so the wind won't cut off your breath."

All that Aaron wasn't, Freddy was. Williams, a suave veteran of the Ed Sullivan show and military-base tours, created both characters and switched between them without taking a breath. The illusion was perfect, even during a three-way phone call with Freddy humming nonchalantly on the side ("Georgia, oh yeah, man"). This was the swing act, long or short depending on how the evening was going, but Williams was never routine. The band was still laughing at his gags, and they had been listening all season.

"So what about that election you always talkin' about," said Freddy.

"For President, don't you care who won?"

"No."

"Why not, Freddy?"

"Sheeit, man, I'm black and I'm poor. I'm gonna catch hell either way!" The house always came down with that line. Freddy dipped his head in acknowledgement.

"Right *on!* Tell the truth, ain't no harm in that!"

Were they not so well documented in plastic, Ray Charles' years at Atlantic would be the legend Jerry Wexler proclaims. After "I Got a Woman" he couldn't miss. From 1954 to 1959 Charles came out with perfect single after perfect single. "Hallelujah I Love Her So" won him many new listeners with its easy-going beat and happy romance—"she brings me coffee in my favorite cup." "This Little Girl of Mine" (based on the gospel song, "This Little Light of Mine"), the gorgeous piano blues of "Sweet Sixteen Bars," the limping rhythm of "Lonely Avenue," the cool of "Get on the Right Track, Baby" (which went back to his first professional days)—all hit. By 1957 the Raelets (then sometimes spelled "Raylettes," and with Marjorie Hendricks in the fore) had appeared, coming into full flower with "Talkin' 'bout You" backed with "What Kind of Man Are You," on which they sing the whole vocal. In 1958, Ray recorded "My Bonnie" ("lies over the ocean"), a bold leap across the barriers of idiom which was swingingly successful.

The powerful "What'd I Say" lifted Ray's popularity to a new plateau. Ray's driving electric piano introduces the song's memorable riff and is met by loud-singing cymbals. The song ends but some angry women protest; Ray cools them out by restarting the groove from a new angle. That pleases the ladies, and they all whoop and grunt out the side together. Twisters loved "What'd I Say" because it was so good to dance to. It sold at hit volumes for years instead of months.

"Hey y'all," Ray sang in his version of Louis Jordan's "Let the Good Times Roll":

Tell everybody, Ray Charles in town
I got a dollar and a quarter
And I'm just rarin' to clown
But don't let no female
Play me cheap
I got fifty cents more than I'm gonna keep
So let the good times roll.*

In comparing Ray Charles to Duke Ellington, Jerry Wexler points out that Ray sings and that the Duke never sold many singles. Ellington had sold many a three-minute 78 rpm disc in the three decades before 1955, but he (and the rest of jazz) had little place in the Top 40. While rock 'n' roll prospered, big bands died like dinosaurs; bop and cool jazz combos eked out livings in a few clubs in the big cities. Like the line between folk and commercial music drawn by devotees in the 1950s, there was a line between jazz and rock 'n' roll. In jazz brilliant instrumentalists led the way; singers imitated the horns. Singers were the heart of rock and R&B; instrumentalists were sidemen in their support. Jazzmen were pure and poor; rhythm stars posed with Cadillacs. Jazzmen made LPs, rockers made 45s. By these standards Ray Charles was rock 'n' roll. Except for a live album from Newport and the *Genius* album issued as he left Atlantic, Ray's LPs of the 1950s were collections of singles. Song and singer were in the foreground. Every note was played for popular appeal. Ray competed successfully for radio time, store shelf space, and the teenager's dollar with Elvis, Roy Orbison, Sam Cooke, Jackie Wilson, Paul Anka, Pat Boone, and Atlantic's own Drifters and Coasters.

Yet no musician or fan could patronize Ray's licks. His playing (alto sax and organ besides piano), arranging, composing, and singing were superb, as swinging as Fletcher Henderson, as sophisticated as the MJQ, as personal and vivid as Louis Armstrong. No one played a funkier blues, and as for laying the message on the people, he was the High Priest, the Right Reverend. Sometimes the papers listed him as a jazz pianist, and at others as a blues vocalist, singer-songwriter, R&B artist, or rock 'n' roll star. At Atlantic Ray Charles became a musical movement unto himself. His career moved parallel to rock 'n' roll but remained independent of it; he imitated no one and was himself inimitable. The most complete musician to master the art of hit making, singing from the directionless darkness of his blindness, he broadcast his music in all directions at once. His communication was as intimate as his audience large.

In 1959 Atlantic supplied the only name that fit: "Genius." It stuck. Ray disowns it in interviews but has himself so announced at every concert. The *Genius* LP was a great success. It showed off Ray the balladeer, singing pop standards like "Come Rain or Come Shine," and surrounded by a full orchestra, choir, and strings, with his regular band supplying the same raw energy it had been delivering for five years previous. Ray's treatment of the tunes was romantically red-blooded. *The Genius of Ray Charles* got played whole on the easy-listening stations, and a new audience learned about Ray Charles.

Ray's last hit single for Atlantic was a Nashville blues, Hank Snow's "I'm Movin' On." That he was. When his Atlantic contract lapsed, he ignored Wexler's entreaties to stay with the company "that made him," and went to a major label as a major star. Why? "This is a business, you know," he said backstage at the Circle Star. "Since one never knows how long one's career is gonna be, one naturally takes advantage of the best opportunities one can get." ABC-Paramount offered an advance fit for a sultan, a star's contract, and a record distribution system with which Atlantic, then still an R&B label, could not compete.

Atlantic consoled itself for the loss by issuing and reissuing everything by Charles it had on tape. More Atlantic LPs by Ray Charles came out after his departure than before it. *Soul Meetin'* with Milt Jackson is jazz-blues at its mellowest; Ray switches between piano and sax. *The Genius After Hours* and *The*

*Genius Sings the Blues* both have previously unreleased material; the others, like *The Ray Charles Story* LPs, are all repackagings. All but *Ray Charles in Person.* Volumes One and Two of the *Story* series are the most comprehensive introduction to Ray's Atlantic years; *In Person* is the most exciting. Charles and his band had never stopped touring, and on May 28, 1959, they gave a concert in Atlanta sponsored by radio station WAOK. Also on the bill were Ruth Brown, Jimmy Reed, B. B. King, Roy Hamilton, and Huey "Piano" Smith and the Clowns. One microphone, a hundred feet from the stage, picked up everything for a portable tape recorder; the sound quality, wrote Zenas Sears, "most studio technicians dream about but never achieve." The audience at Herndon Stadium had been whipped up by hours of blues before Ray came on. He drove them wild. He did "The Right Time," "What'd I Say," "Yes Indeed," and "Tell the Truth" in generously long and cooking versions. He made "Drown in My Own Tears" a six-minute epic. The band, which sounds as full as one twice its seven-man size, stars in "Frenesi," Marjorie Hendricks in "Tell the Truth," Ray on every track. He comes through like gangbusters, shouting to the band, to the delirious audience, and to himself. Clearly delighted to be on stage, he sounds confident on the record, his voice strong and free. Whenever he feels like it, he shouts with his throat wide open. "I wanna know don't it make you feel alright!"

Except for the weekend, when the Circle Star had two shows daily, Ray flew back to LA after each concert and came back the next evening. His band and B. B. King's band stayed at two motels near the theater. B. B. was at the Fairmont in San Francisco. Ray went back to LA to work: he was mixing down a new single for the Raelets and selecting one for himself as well. He got to the Circle Star each night about eight, a good two hours before he would go on. Taylor drove him from the airport in a yellow rented Toronado, pulling into a reserved spot just beside the stage door. The nights were damp and cold—a spell of freezing weather that broke Bay Area records was beginning. One night we met them there. Ray stepped out of the car, reached into the back seat for a black overcoat, and slipped it across his broad shoulders. Tall and of imposing build, he has weighed 165 pounds since he was eighteen. Touring, he says, keeps him in shape. With sight he might have been an athlete or dancer like three other Robinsons—Sugar Ray, Jackie, and Bill "Mr. Bojangles." He groped and fumbled for a moment before he found the button to lock the car door, then slammed it shut, and stood rocking slightly back on his heels. Taylor came around the car, gave Ray his arm, and led his boss in. Ray moved like a man used to being in the dark; his head hung forward, his stance suggested patience and caution. In contrast, his stage manner is uninhibited, almost flailing; there he knows where he is and what he's doing, and is reacting to how he sounds.

Taylor led Charles through the crowded and smoky back-stage to the star's dressing room. After he had Ray settled, Taylor reemerged and invited us—a lady photographer and myself—in for the interview. Ray was sitting when we entered but stood up as we were introduced, holding out his hand for us to shake.

"Jes a second before we start," he said in an easy drawl. "Bob, what they got on the menu for tonight?" Taylor read a list of entrees; Ray didn't like the sound of any of them.

"Tomorrow's special is filet of sole. You like that," said Taylor.

"Yeah, *tomorrow,*" said Ray. "See if they'll rib me up some of that sole *tonight.* Now," turning to us, "what's on your mind?"

We told him how much we liked his music. "I appreciate that," he said with a gracious bow of his head. I wanted to find out how he made his LPs. How and to what end had he picked the songs, the sounds? "Whatever I'm doing, I try for what sounds good to me. I don't do anything special. We lay down the tracks, mostly I do the rhythm and the band and voices at one time, add the strings and maybe a few horns later—pretty simple. I've been doing most of my own engineering and mixing for a pretty good while now. I have some idea of what I'm trying to hear, but it's just a matter of taste, what the ears hear. It is something I can't explain. Asking about it is like asking what is love. It's something you just have to have a feel for yourself.

"The whole thing with an album for me," he said, dropping the *l* so it came out *ah-bum*, "is deciding what kind of theme I can come up with. There's all kinds of material, no shortage of songs for me to sing. I select songs I feel I can sing. A lot of good songs I can't make work for me. If a song fits what I'm doing and I can do it, okay. I mean, man," and suddenly his face had a big smile on it, "there's nothing in them ahbums that's gonna shake the world, I *assure* you. Ray Charles is all right, but there *are* other people in this world."

Who, I asked him, had sung the line "Me too" in response to his "I like that" on "Every Saturday Night" on *Volcanic Action of My Soul*. "You mean on 'Take Me Home, Country Roads'?" He laughed. "That was me talking to myself on another track." The conversation drifted on. Among classical composers he said he liked Chopin and Beethoven. Both, like himself, were masters of the piano. "Beethoven—on many things—had very, *very* much feeling in what he did." In general he said he inclined to "sentimental" music, nothing "too serious."

No, he had no idea how big a seller *Volcanic Action of My Soul* was. "Not as big as *Message from the People*, I'm sure of that. Man, that album, if you can't get the theme of that album, you ain't listening. It's all there. I feel that there are many things to be corrected here, but I also feel this is the hippest country in the world." He said he doesn't make his LPs all at once. He thinks of songs to do, does them when he can, and then groups them in albums as he sees fit. A portable chess set sat on the table beside him; he was in the middle of a game with Taylor. Charles said he had no favorite album: "When I'm making them, they all sound good. It's all what knocks me out at the time. I go through a million emotions with each one."

As we talked, Taylor stood in the background arranging Ray's tuxedos in a small closet. Ray sat comfortable in an easy chair, dressed in a brown-on-brown shirt and a brown jacket and

slacks. He waved his hands to make points or held them together in his lap. His temples were touched with a distinguished
bit of grey, and his brown face was relaxed and unlined. Withal
Ray Charles is a most handsome man. "I mean, certain days you
feel certain ways, then you feel something else the next day.
Doesn't stop, you know?" A waiter arrived with the grilled filet
of sole, and the interview ended. We all stood, and Ray put out
his hand again. Thank you, we said, and so did he. He squeezed
my hand with a mute warmth that surprised me. "God bless
you, darlin," he said to the lady photographer, shaking her hand
between both of his. "That's life, isn't it?" he said, continuing
his thought. "First one thing, then another."

"Every day, every day I have the blues." B. B. King, in a
midnight blue tuxedo, leaned forward from the waist. His head
was cocked back, his eyes were closed, and his eyebrows were
arched up as high as his agile facial muscles could take them. He
plucked one note on his guitar. Tweeenng. Otherwise complete
silence. Another note, this one a little higher. Tweeeng-ng.
Again—tweeen-ng-ng. When he plucked the fourth time, the
"eeeng" did not stop or fade but grew. He shifted his glossy
brown electric Gibson slightly, holding it firmly to his body with
his right forearm and elbow. As the note grew it changed from
the electrically amplified image of the vibrating string into the
hollow whine of feedback. Feedback occurs when the amplified
sound is "fed back" into the amplifying system (for example,
when a live mike is held too close to a loudspeaker), thus getting
boosted again and again until it puts the amplifier into a frenzy
of which it wailingly complains. B. B. kept the wail and controlled the frenzy. Slowly the feedback devoured the original
note. Behind him the band started riffing gently. B. B. twisted
his body and the guitar with it; the feedback howl rose, perfectly in tune. How long could he keep it going? The band built
to a climax. The note continued; the band faded away, and
when all was again silent, B. B. let the note fade also. Just before
it was gone he chopped it off with a quick chord, the band came

in with a showy finale, and the song was over. B. B. bowed low to the tumultuous applause.

Baritone saxophonist Lewis Hubert introduced B. B. the same way every night ("Let's hear it for a young man who's making quite a name for himself"); every night B. B. was spectacular. Success with white audiences in the late 1960s gave King, like John Lee Hooker, a new career. He has responded with vigor to its challenges. He has had several big hits ("The Thrill Is Gone" was a smash) and has played all the TV shows and clubs he dreamed of when laboring on the chitlin circuit. B. B.'s act was polished, his band snappily dressed (Ray's sidemen were openly envious of their purple and scarlet uniforms), and his playing dramatically free and experimental. The tunes hadn't changed: "Worry, Worry," "How Blue Can You Get," and "It's My Own Fault," were still his staples. His shouts were bull roars, his picking soulful and studious.

B. B. was proud of his band, Sonny Freeman and the Unusuals, and introduced them with care every night. On piano Ron Levy from Boston; Milton Hopkins, rhythm guitar, from East Palo Alto, California; "Little Joe" Burton, trombone, Chicago; trumpeter Eddie Roe, Shreveport, Louisiana. The saxes: Hubert ("He's the big spender of the group," said B. B.), from Tampa, Florida; alto Cato Walker ("the baby, been with us one month"), Memphis; and Bobby Forte ("the lover—at least he *says* so"), tenor, Oakland, Cal. On bass was Wilbert Freeman, Detroit, and on drums was the ever-smiling Sonny Freeman, who had been with B. B. for fifteen years. "Now some of you may wonder, if a man and a woman find it hard to stay together that long, how can two men do it?" said B. B. "Well don't look at us funny, honey! Seriously though, he's a good friend and a fine musician, Sonny Freeman, give him a hand." Sonny stood up at that and waved his sticks, but he was still hard to see behind his large brass cymbals. B. B. said this was the first time for him at the Circle Star, and he wasn't sure the people were used to his blues, "but I hope if you don't go away fans, at least you'll go away friends." He was happy to be there, especially to be on the bill with the Genius—"they ought to be charging *me* admission, I dig his music so."

Then he was into another tune. He started simply, flicking notes from high on the neck. "You need someone," he sang, "someone who really cares for you." Bobby Forte's tenor filled the silences with round lusty notes and sudden twisting runs. Sonny Freeman tapped steadily at his high hat, his right foot kept up a muffled thumping from his bass drum. "And that someone," sang Riley B. King, Indianola, Mississippi, his eyes closed, a sideways grin across his mug, both his index fingers pointing to his heart, "that someone is me, me, me, me, me, me, me."

Ray's first single for ABC-Paramount, "My Baby," came out on the company's AmPar label. It was not a hit, nor was the second, "Sticks and Stones." The third was "Georgia" in August, 1960. It sold one and a half million copies. The album that it inspired, *Genius on the Road,* in which Ray toured the country via "Alabamy Bound," "Moonlight in Vermont," "Blue Hawaii," and the like, sold 750,000 copies. ABC had made a good deal for itself.

"We felt he had a bright future," said Sam Clark, then president of the label, "profitable for him and profitable for us, if he moved from the idiom he was in at the time to what we saw as a potential for him." That is, cross over from rock 'n' roll to the lucrative "pop field"—the market which had been *the* popular market for music until rock 'n' roll. In the 1940s everything but pop had been a specialty market; pop was the Establishment, dominated by the major labels, the publishing companies, and the licensing guild, ASCAP. The rise of the indies, with their regional and racial flavors, the declining importance of sheet-music sales relative to record sales and airplay, and BMI's consequent success in signing up new writers and publishers outside ASCAP's monopoly—all cut deep into pop's hegemony. By 1960 pop was but one of many idioms, best defined by what it was not—not C&W, R&B, rock 'n' roll, jazz, folk, classical.

However beset by challengers, pop maintained its respectability, and if to some it seemed bland, it had the solid financial base of massive public acceptance. A conservative common denominator, pop music was the acme for artists who appealed to the average American in every American. Bing Crosby was Christmas, Guy Lombardo New Year's. Perry Como, Connie Francis, Eddie Fisher, Al Hirt, Eydie Gorme, Jo Stafford, Dinah Shore, Frankie Laine, Nelson Riddle, and Teresa Brewer were members of the family at a time when Little Richard was not a fit topic at polite dinner tables. Lawrence Welk was pop's goody-goody, Frank Sinatra its brilliant bad boy. Pop's repertory of songs touched all bases but drew most heavily from Broadway shows, Hollywood movies, and the high Tin Pan Alley tradition of the Gershwins, Irving Berlin, Rodgers and Hart, Cole Porter, Harold Arlen, and Jerome Kern. RCA Victor, Capitol, Decca, and Columbia were pop labels. ABC-Paramount, owned by the radio-TV broadcasting network and the Paramount movie theater chain, was a newcomer in pop's mainstream—only five years old in 1960. Later in the sixties the company signed B. B. King and Curtis Mayfield's Impressions; Impulse, its jazz subsidiary, presented Duke Ellington, John Coltrane, and Count Basie in lavish albums. More typical were LPs like *Chris Connor Now!, Love Is a Guitar,* and Frank de Vol singing *The New Old Sweet Songs.*

Clark's corporate pride notwithstanding, Ray's celebrated turn to pop had begun musically at Atlantic, and though the paper label in the middle of the discs had changed, what was in the spiral groove was still 100 percent Ray Charles. ABC A&R man Sid Feller, like Jerry Wexler before him, was there to help and to see that nothing went wrong. Ray liked and trusted him, and the two men still work together. Ray's records, Feller has written, "have all been done exactly as he wanted them, right down to the last note of the arrangement." ABC encouraged and facilitated Ray's urge to go beyond the limits of jazz and R&B both in the studio and in the selling of the product. The Erteguns and Wexler, aesthetically committed to

R&B and disdainful (until the late sixties) of pop, with no experience, few connections, and only scanty distribution in the pop market, could not have been as helpful. "Georgia" was a sensation, a ballad exquisitely, nakedly rendered. Ray sings and plays with an aching filled with knowledge and loss. The strings rise and fall with the flow of his recollections; the echoing choir emphasizes his loneliness. Brushed drums and a solemn walking bass keep a mournful rhythm. During the week of November 14 to 21, 1960, it was a number one on *Billboard*'s national chart, Ray's first single to reach the top.

A year later "Hit the Road, Jack" was on top for two weeks. Percy Mayfield wrote the song (and "Danger Zone," the haunting blues which was the 45's B-side), the same Mayfield who, when Ray was starting out in Seattle, was a star whose deft and often humorous touch Ray admired. They had collaborated on "Tell Me How Do You Feel" when Ray was at Atlantic; by 1961 Charles had started his own publishing company, Tangerine Music (after his favorite fruit), and Mayfield was one of its writers. He has contributed dozens of songs to Tangerine. "Hit the Road, Jack" was the company's first hit. Millions, myself included, turned the car radio all the way up when it came on. A lady is kicking Ray out, and she's not fooling. Her "don't you come back no more no no more no more no more" rises against the song's repetitive descending bass line. Could any woman be so mean? Ray can hardly believe it, but, "I guess if you say so, I better pack my things and go." "That's right," sings the lady, "Hit the road, Jack!" You can almost hear the rolling pin in her hand.

Ray's second ABC LP, *Dedicated to You,* was all about girls —"Hardhearted Hannah," "Ruby," "Stella by Starlight," and others. Impulse put out *Genius + Soul = Jazz,* with Ray on organ leading Count Basie's band through ten swingers, including "One Mint Julep." It was number twenty-seven on *Cashbox*'s Top Albums of 1961, high for a jazz LP. Next was a volume of duets with Betty Carter. Then, as Rick Ward eventually wrote in the liner notes, "Sid Feller . . . received a telephone call from Ray Charles, who asked for the top country and western hits of the past twenty years. Completely confused and wondering what possible use Ray could make of such material, Sid immediately began collecting songs." The result: *Modern Sounds in Country and Western Music.* "Yep!" cries Ray to open it, and the band and Raelets rock into an uptempo version of the Everly Brothers' hit, "Bye, Bye Love." Eddy Arnold's "You Don't Know Me," done tenderly, follows, then "Half As Much," "I Love You So Much It Hurts," and a quick "Just a Little Lovin'." The side ends with "Born to Lose," Ray singing with particular delicacy, backed by strings and voices. This was the B-side of the single released from the album; "I Can't Stop Loving You," a song by Don Gibson, was the A-side. Total sales of the 45 now equal about three million; it was an immediate smash and topped the *Billboard* charts for the whole month of June, 1962. The LP was Ray's first gold record, another successful declaration of musical independence.

*Modern Sounds* is an honest title. The repertory and sound are true country and western. Ray hadn't forgotten a thing from his days yodeling with the Florida Playboys. He captures all the bittersweet in Hank Williams' "You Win Again." "I once was blind but now I see," he sings in the old country song, "Careless Love." The LP ends on a bouncy note, Ray's voice climbing to the stratosphere, with Williams' "Hey Good Lookin'." Yet David "Fathead" Newman's tenor solos, Ray's own rambunctious piano, his lush use of the Marty Paich Strings, and the full horns were all unprecedented in country music. Drums had been allowed on stage at the Grand Ole Opry only since the mid-fifties, and Nashville producers were still cautious of offending their tradition-minded audience with anything too slick or citified. Opry fans loved the album. A hit is always influential in the music business, and the modernization of the Nashville Sound proceeded apace in the mid-sixties.

The follow-up album, *Modern Sounds Vol. Two,* contained dazzling versions of "You Are My Sunshine," Gibson's "Oh Lonesome Me," and Williams' "Your Cheating Heart." It sold well for a sequel; at the same time a *Greatest Hits* collection was becoming a million-seller. In 1964 Ray had another single hit with "Busted": "I'm broke, no bread, I mean like nothing, forget it!" Ten years after "I Got a Woman," what new worlds had he to conquer? He had won every award, some of them two and three times. Europe had received him deliriously. In his honor the Paris Mint struck a coin with these words in French braille: "I want people to feel my soul."

His wish had been fulfilled. Many loved everything he did; many more had been touched by something of his, whether it was "Takes Two to Tango," "Old Man River," "California Here I Come," "Them That Got," or "Mess Around." Mention his name to your friends: one remembers seeing him at Blinstrubs in Boston on her sixteenth birthday, another saw him at the Palais des Sports in Paris, a third sneaked into a black-only concert in Houston, a fourth has a battered copy of *Genius Sings the Blues*, precious because it was his only record for years. "My brother, he loved Ray Charles," says a fifth. "His favorite song was 'Mary Ann.'" I like the way he sings about "a greenback dollar bill, little piece of paper, coated with chlorophyll."

"You can take any song and put it in any idiom you want," Ray has said. He makes it sound easy. Musical idiom begins, like custom, accents, and even language, in the resemblance of our physical gestures to those of the people around us. There is mountain music and flatland music, Spanish music and German music, music of country and town. Most musicians play their instruments idiomatically just as most Swedes use their vocal chords to speak Swedish. The musical world organizes itself by idiom, from the classical piano teacher with his group of pupils to the club that features Latin bands "Fri. and Sat. nites," from the Nashville tour promoter to the "soft rock" producer on the Strip in LA. In the same month that I saw Ray Charles, I heard Earl Scruggs and Artur Rubenstein. Both played with utmost freedom and expressiveness a wide variety of music within idioms which they have enriched with their lives.

Ray Charles has made a career of transcending idiom, ignoring its limits while delighting in the variety of evocative effects it gives to his music. He does not learn different idioms to switch between them, but continually enlarges his personal idiom by a process of sonic absorption. *"Everything* makes a sound," he told Whitney Balliett. "You have to train yourself to pay attention all the time." Listening in directionless darkness he hears the background music of the world around him, the songs that, as Chuck Berry has said, "you don't really hear." These popular sounds, musical zephyrs once called airs, are the stuff of Ray's music. Each one communicates specific emotions with word and melody. Ray does not care where they come from; if a song moves him, "if I can get the feeling out of it," he will sing it back into the darkness.

Ray started to close "The Long and Winding Road." He had sung the song, written by Paul McCartney, in earnest tones, emphasizing each word, making big blocks of notes on the piano. Certain phrases had jumped out clearly: "pool of tears," "many times I've been alone," "the long I said *winding* road." "It leads me to your door," he sang in ending. "Road, please take me home, take me home." The applause was rising. Ray stopped singing and talked to himself off-mike. "Yeah, take me home, have mercy, yeah, amen to *that."*

He had reached the middle of his show opening night at the Circle Star. As he would on succeeding nights, he took the opportunity to break the flow of music with some chit-chat. "This is what I call stalling," he said "taking a break without you folks noticing." Two sound men tiptoed up onto the stage behind him to move a mike stand. "Whatcha doin' back there?" said Ray. "I like you out front where I can see you."

The band sat quietly in the pit: Mike Conlon let the spit out of his trumpet, Steve Turre flipped through the pages of the thick music notebook on his stand. "I feel a *feeling* in here tonight," Ray said. "Anybody seen what the moon looks like outside?" "Yeah," shouted a young man in a front row, "it's square."

"And so are you!" Ray shot back. "You know, it's funny. You hire somebody to do something for you, let 'em do it. Here I am, entertaining you, you've come out and paid your money for me to work for you, but there's always somebody who wants to entertain me. Damn! And then there's photographers. I'd like to see a law that would make people get a license to own cameras. Some photographers wait til just when I'm getting to a nice quiet spot, then—click click click—man, it's like you were working on your job and somebody sticks you in the rear end with an ice pick." His gripes off his chest, he went on.

"Okay, now at this point in the show, I want to ask you to do something for me." His voice became sexy and confiding. "In a few minutes five young ladies are gonna walk out here and, well, you know how ladies are . . ." He paused until there were a few laughs from the audience, then added an insinuating "heh heh heh" of his own.

"They like to be appreciated, to be told how pretty they are, how nice they look. Now these young ladies are very pretty." He stopped; the audience waited for him to go on. He laughed. "I can *hear* you wondering, asking yourselves, 'How can *he* tell that?' You're thinking, 'I thought he couldn't see.' Well, maybe I can't see, but I can *feel*. I don't know about eyesight, but the sense of touch is wonderful, yes, Lord!"

"Right on!" responded a dozen or more voices. "Have mercy," said Ray. "I bet some of you are thinking, 'There goes Ray, talking about *it* again.' I'm getting to be an old man now, but I still say—since *it* brought me here, let *it* take me away!

"So I want you to help me welcome my little darlings, my sweethearts, God bless 'em. I don't care what you do; you can stomp your feet, clap your hands together, whistle, shout, but whatever you do, do it loud, as loud as you can. Okay? All right, let's welcome these fine young ladies, everybody, the Rae-*lets!*"

Five women walked quickly down the aisle from the dressing room and up the ramp to the stage. They were in floor-length gowns of pastel chiffon—pale greens, pinks, and yellows in gauzy swirls. Their necklines and the cuffs of their full sleeves were encrusted with spangles. First was Mabel John, the leader of the group and sister of the late "Little Willie" John Davenport, the author of "Fever," who died in federal prison in 1967. Sister Mabel had traveled all over the world as a blues singer with her brother's band, the Upsetters (Milton Hopkins, now with B.B., was the guitar player). "When my brother passed," she said one night backstage, "Ray called up and asked me if I'd head up a new set of Raelets. We're the fourth group of Raelets. We spell it 'Raelets' because Ray is for a man, Rae is the way a lady spells it." She is a short woman with a matronly and confident air.

Behind Mabel came tiny Susaye Greene, her hair pulled into one pigtail that stuck up straight from the top of her head. Then Vernita Moss, a big girl with a voice to match, curly-headed Estella Yarbrough, then Dorothy Berry. (The Raelets have most often been a quartet, but Sister Dorothy fit in so well when Sister Estella was sick for the 1971 season that she was kept on for 1972.) They got the ovation Ray had asked for, and rightly so: they were as beautiful as he had described. They stood straight and smiled, eyes beaming.

In their solo portion of the show the Raelets had done R&B hits—Aretha's "Rock Steady" and "Chain of Fools," Sam and Dave's "Hold On, I'm Coming"—plus secular songs that bordered on gospel. In "West of Eden" they sang that they saw "new horizons—in my soul, in my bones, in my mind"; in "Bad Water" they urged, "Let's plan instead of dreaming." With Ray on stage their role was supportive, but they gave up not a whit of their independence. "Listen to that man, girls," said Mabel when he got a mite fresh. "What *is* he saying?" replied Vernita. "Same old thing," said Susaye. When not singing they stood together casually; during the songs they moved with an even undulation. The chiffon billowed in clouds about them. They looked like angels.

"All right!" said Ray. "Have mercy," said the Raelets. The stall was over. They began a song with a short repetitive groove. The girls' job was to sing, "Feel it, yes, I feel it," pause for a few measures, then sing it again, continuing as long as Ray kept the groove going. Meanwhile, Ray improvised lines to fit the pause and the Raelets' response. "Can you feel it," he started, "when it's late at night and you're all alone can you—" and the women sang, "Feel it, yes, I feel it." "When the music grabs you down in your soul can you—" "Feel it, yes, I feel it."

The "it" became himself. "Can you feel me, feel me, feel me?" The ladies could. "Can you feel, aw, not so much me, as feel my heart?" "Feel it, yes, I feel it." "But do you *feel* it?" They did. "Oh, do you feel it, mama—" Ray's voice became serious, even worried, "You wouldn't be lyin' to me now, would you, mama?" Ray hoped everybody there might feel it, yes, feel it. "Even those reporters out there when they write about us I hope they—" He said it felt good to feel it, felt young to feel it, and that anybody could feel it.

Finally he ended it. "I *felt* that," he said laughing. "Ain't no harm in saying what the truth is." He began to play the piano, firm and vigorous chords. The band and the Raelets knew the song he was beginning and readied themselves. "I got something in my bones, make me want to shout hallelujah," he sang. "Lift every voice and sing," sang the Raelets. The song was a hymn to music, to the glory of universal harmony, and Ray and his ensemble rocked through it like they meant it. To introduce the next song Ray said, "As long as breath keeps me alive, this is my theme." The Raelets came in, "I can't stop loving you." Half the crowd did its best to join in. "They say that time," Ray sang,

> Heals a broken heart
> But time has stood still
> Since we've been apart.*

The next song that night was "Look What They've Done to My Song, Ma," a hit by a young singer called Melanie; Ray recorded it on *Message from the People*. The band kept up a blaring pace, and Ray shouted out the words. "Look what they done to my song, ma," he sang. "What is it, son?" responded Sister Vernita. "They put it in a plastic bag, shaked it all upside down. . . . They're driving me insane. . . . It isn't what they done to my song, it's what they're trying to do to me." At moments he sounded angry, but by the end he was vowing, "I'm gonna keep on workin', working on the buildin', mama, just like you told me, mama."

Applause faded again to silence. Ray played the piano. Once, then twice, then a third time, it seemed that he was going to begin a new song. Each time his hands and mind changed direction. The band, the Raelets, and the audience listened and waited. The piano rang sombrely. Wry dissonances flashed and disappeared. Ray played on for a full three minutes. Then he was done. "Sister Susaye, if you will, please." With this cue the other four Raelets walked over to the piano, leaving Susaye alone at the mike. Ray gave her a short introduction, and she began to sing "Over the Rainbow."

She sang it like a true blue diva. The delicate bones of her jaw and face were revealed by the supple movements the notes required, which stretched the smooth tan skin of her face and neck. Her eyes were wide open and glistened. She stood rooted on one spot, but her arms rose and fell, her whole body churned with an earnest excitement. She had looked different coming in to work that night in dark glasses, a long grey fur coat, her breasts swinging free under a silk T-shirt. Susaye Greene, successful soprano from New York City, had become Sister Susaye; her sophistication became the innocence the song required. The words came out clear. Somewhere over the rainbow there was a land remembered only from lullabies, a land higher than the chimney tops, far beyond the clouds. There bluebirds flew —Sister Susaye's fingers, with long painted nails, fluttered like the birds her voice created. Ray accompanied her; the band was silent except for bass and drums. If those "little tiny birds" could fly so far beyond the rainbow to that golden land, asked Sister Susaye, readying herself to go clear to the top of her range,

"Why oh why can't I?" She held the final syllable, splitting it into a dozen curlicues, each one higher than the last. She finished with her heels off the stage.

"Now you have *heard* it," said Ray as the house broke into wild cheering. Sister Susaye smiled and bowed. The four other Raelets walked back to join her.

For Ray Charles the middle and late 1960s lacked the public drama of the previous decade's sweeping upward curve. Show-biz headlines featured the rise of younger talents—Aretha Franklin, Otis Redding, Wilson Pickett, James Brown, Motown, the Beatles, the Rolling Stones, and Bob Dylan; there was no new way to praise the Genius. If the image was fixed, the man kept moving, continuing and consolidating.

Ray had found an invaluable aide in Joe Adams. Adams had been a black pioneer in network radio—"the first Negro coast-to-coast." His voice is still smoothly theatrical. In 1959 Charles hired him as a master of ceremonies, to give the show, Adams has said, "a little dignity." One night Adams noticed that stage crews never varied the lighting during Ray's performance. "I imagine that people had been taking advantage of the fact that Ray Charles is blind," Adams has written. He plotted out light-ing, audience response leapt up, and an appreciative Ray made him his right-hand man.

Together they built a headquarters, the RPM Building in West Los Angeles, convenient to Ray's home and the airport. The building had room for Ray to become what he describes as a "small businessman." He employs about forty people, half of them musicians. In the RPM building are firms to handle every aspect of Ray's work—touring, song publishing, talent manage-ment, and record production. But RPM's heart is its studio. Ray began recording there in 1964; his *Country and Western Meets Rhythm and Blues,* in 1965, was the first album done entirely on home ground. The one that followed, *Crying Time,* bore the legend, "Produced by the Tangerine Record Corporation," and Tangerine's logo, a large *T* with *R* and *C* in smaller, entwined letters. A few LPs later the legend read, "A Product of the Tangerine Record Corporation." Ray's control of the medium had become as complete as it needed to be: he could now make the tapes, have them pressed in Columbia's pressing plant, and deliver them to ABC (which by the 1970s had dropped Paramount, moved to LA, and become ABC-Dunhill) to distribute.

After a brief marriage to a girl who went home once too often for him, Ray married again in the mid-fifties. In the mid-sixties he and Della Robinson had three boys growing up in their big house in LA's View Park. Ray toured by private plane; the alternation of touring and home seasons became an established pattern. In 1965 Ray put down heroin. He had used the drug steadily all his professional life, since shortly after his parents died. Several brushes with the law made it clear that continued use would threaten his whole career. Faced with a similar choice thirty years earlier, Louis Armstrong had bidden a fond farewell to his beloved Maryjane. Ray hospitalized himself for three months, then took a year's rest. Since then he has refused to express any regret for taking heroin, commenting only that for him the drug had become a dead end.

In the decade after "I Can't Stop Loving You" he had no hit as big. Every record made money, however. He has an enviably solid audience; they and the thousands who find they have to have *this* record have made Tangerine a company to bank on. He has scored with a veteran's reliability in the 45 market. He turned Buck Owens' tearjerker, "Crying Time," into a soul ballad and had a hit with it. His next was "Together Again," and he followed it with the magnificent "Let's Go Get Stoned." He brought out all the sex in "Makin' Whoopee"; the B-side was a piano version of the same stand-by—both sides were hits. His dreamily slurred "Yesterday" was a hit; he followed with another Paul McCartney song, "Eleanor Rigby," another hit. In 1971 he did the swinging country tune "Don't Change on Me" and rode high on the pop and C&W charts again.

He started losing the critics in the late sixties. Some didn't like his success, some didn't like his material, and some even didn't like the way he sang. They found his new albums wanting when compared to his early ones. "No matter what they write in the paper tomorrow, I'm playing here tonight," Ray said once. As for the albums, they were getting better and better. The texture of his music was becoming slowly richer, its effects ever more exquisite. His musical understanding broadened with every new song he did, and each of the thousands of times he sang the old ones taught him something. His progress from Swingtime to Atlantic to ABC to Tangerine had given him a top-to-bottom knowledge of the medium. By 1970 Ray Charles had become a record maker supreme.

In the late 1960s, for Ray and for the rest of the popular music world, LPs became more important than singles, but he did not forget the strength of a short and likeable song as an LP's basic ingredient. His first attempts to group songs into albums that held together were straightforward—place songs, girl songs, duets, C&W, jazz, happy songs, sad songs, a live album. *Ingredients in a Recipe for Soul*, 1963, which included "That Lucky Old Sun," "Old Man River," and "Busted" was his first LP with no obvious grouping to the tunes except the fact of being pressed in the same piece of plastic. *Ray's Moods* in 1966 was similarly eclectic; its title, like many subsequent ones, indicated only the source and variety of the contents.

A picture of Ray's face is on nearly every album cover. Dark glasses cover his eyes like the mask of the Lone Ranger. I haven't heard all his albums—there are over thirty, not counting collections. Listening to most of them in sequence I was impressed with Ray's steadily increasing mastery in presenting the album itself as a musical experience. The early LPs may be compared to books of fine photographs; the later albums are like films. At first fixed mikes recorded the band to sound like a stage ensemble with soloists; gradually Ray started mixing his sounds so that this aural imitation of visual experience disappears. He calls up sounds at will—electric guitar, horns, strings, voices—and they recede when their moment is past. The ever-shifting instrumentation creates a flow of musical moods with the same magic that makes film images move.

*Crying Time*, 1966, opens with the title song; Ray's girl is leaving. In the next song, "No Use Crying," she's gone. Ray screams on organ. He gets drunk in "Let's Go Get Stoned." "Going Down Slow" is the story of a juicer on his deathbed. He asks for "Peace of Mind" in the next cut, and ends the side with "Tears." The Raelets sing the last line: "No more tears, no more tears, I'll spend the rest of my life loving you." A long version of the old "Driftin' Blues" dominates side two. Ray slips in a song by Percy Mayfield ("I call you Mister, and I shine your shoes, you're always laughing when I sing the blues. . . . You think you're so wise, you're in for a big surprise") in which strings, exaggeratedly light, contrast with the pointed lyrics. The next song takes the same idea into the man-woman arena, "You're Just About to Lose Your Clown." He ends with "You've Got a Problem"—five in the morning, nerves jangling, cigarettes gone, walking the floor, and where is she? "You've got a problem, a great big problem, there's nothing that you can do!"

*Ray Charles Invites You to Listen*, 1967, opens with gypsy violins; they are playing "She's Funny That Way." He sings it in a restrained falsetto, as if he were whispering tenderly in the listener's ear. "How Deep Is the Ocean" is smooching slow; "You Made Me Love You" is upbeat jazz—"Listen!" shouts Ray. A tiny electric guitar keeps metronomic rhythm in the honey-like "I'll Be Seeing You." Ray's voice is all over the place but always in the right place at the right time. He sings, "I'll be looking at the moon," like a coyote. Flip the record and—"Here We Go Again." There is a continuity to the record—a muskily intimate mood—that creates a suspense about itself. Where will it go next? "When you look up and make believe," Ray sings in a sudden penetrating tone. Many of the songs I already know; Ray does them as I never heard them before. I have never thought of them together; on Ray's record they caress each other like silk and skin. His bold piano introduction to the Gershwins' "Love Walked In" is an entrance worthy of a lover. The end of the record is Barbra Streisand's smash hit, "People." Ray's happy falsetto shrieks of "Peee-pul!" offset with many baritone "yeahs," make a down-to-earth comedy of Barbra's melodrama.

*Doing His Thing,* 1969, presents ten songs by Jimmy Lewis, a Tangerine Music songwriter. The opening tune is "The Same Thing That Can Make You Laugh Can Make You Cry;" the other songs illustrate that proposition. In 1970 Ray split engineering credit for *Love Country Style* with Tangerine's resident engineer, David Braithewaite. On Johnny Cash's "Ring of Fire" Ray's low monotone suggests John Lee Hooker. "Love is a burning thing," Ray sings, ending in a hoarse whisper against strings, "burns, burns, burns, your ring of fire burns, uh, uh, uh." Transitions are effortless; sound melts into "Don't Change on Me." His voice is commanding; no matter what setting he is in or what role he takes, Ray is instantly recognizable, dependably *there.* He guides the listener through the record. "My world is like a river," he sings, "dark as it is deep." A woman answers him, "Your laughter is like a river." He closes with "Show Me the Sunshine"—"Suddenly you came to me darling, and you changed my world with your first hello."

I could feel my ears opening when I first heard the sublime *Volcanic Action of My Soul* in 1971. Into this black plastic disc Ray Charles has cut a groove of the most extraordinary intensity and common sense. Ray thanks the Lord for the sense of touch; *Volcanic Action* is the sculpture of a blind man. In this dramatic and subtle aural creation are expressed a penetrating and sympathetic humanity, an intelligence of breadth and patience, a humorous and sensual vigor—the qualities of a master.

"If y'all will listen to this, uh, uh, I just wanna tell you people, unnhh, can you hear me now, oooh, I wanna tell all you people out there, I wanna tell all you people just how I feel, oh, how I feel, I feel so *bad*—uh, like a ballgame on a rainy day," he sings. Ray Charles aims *Volcanic Action* directly at me, riveting my attention with his presence. "Many times I've been alone, many times I've cried." He communicates his emotions so well that my spontaneous response is complete empathy. He sings "The Three Bells," the old song about a village deep in a valley where little Jimmy Brown was born, got married, and passed away as "all the chapel bells were ringing." Ray and a choir sing the story simply; the music swells and fades with the flow of Jimmy's life. The last lonely bell rings. "Farewell, Jimmy, we all loved you son," Ray cries. The choir builds to a climax with "May his soul find its salvation in that great eternal love." When the song seems over Ray adds a quiet spoken coda: "Jimmy, you were a friend of mine. I'm sorry, Jimmy."

"Another Dream," Ray sings to open the record: it is like a dream. Ray Robinson took full credit for the engineering; sounds glide past each other like ice skaters. On "Wichita Lineman," as Ray is "singing in the wires," a pedal steel guitar evokes the gleaming curves of railroad tracks. His piano notes in George Harrison's "Something" splash like pebbles in water: "You're asking me will my love grow. I don't know, I don't know." Moods form and dissolve with the sounds. In Jimmy Webb's "See You Then," Ray is alone, running from his woman, "lost forever," and he plays a long stark piano solo. He's surging with happiness as he opens side two with "All I Ever Need Is You." A banjo rollicks throughout and in the middle, after an explosive drum break, a sax blows free over brass. "I May Be Wrong (But I Think You're Wonderful)" is a gas. A boldly mixed conga slaps out the rhythm, and Ray plays with his voice: "Did you hear me, baby, listen here . . . I'm in love, love, love, love, wooooh, Lord, c'mere, talk to me, baby, lets get together, I may be wrong today, but I'll be *right* tonight." He closes the album with "Down in the Valley." It is a song for the campfire when the night's music is in all ears. Ray's version is slow and lonesome. "Hang your head over, and hear the wind blow," sighs the chorus. Ray moans like trees in a summer storm.

*Message from the People*, 1972, is music about this country and its music. "May we forever stand true to our God and to our native land," Ray and a chorus sing in "Lift Up Every Voice and Sing." Then his voice howls with the loner's misery: "I gotta do wrong before they notice me. . . . If I'm crazy, who's to blame." He paints vignettes of dozens of loners—the homeless child, the soldier, the man who gives the soldier his gun, "the boy who won't reach twenty-one," the black man, the white man—then asks heaven to help them, "Help us all when we fall, hear our call." Ray shouts, "I want everybody in the sound of my voice to fall on their knees tonight and pray."

"There'll be no songs to sing, no bells to ring," he sings, "without all men as one." (Backstage at the Circle Star Ray Charles said he hadn't realized so many of the songs he has recorded recently refer to sound and music. "I see what you're talking about, though," he said.) The side closes with a message from Ray to the powers that be that they better listen to the people. "Don't you hear 'em? Don't you hear em? Well then, I feel sorry for you if you don't! . . . Rich or poor, a man is still a man." The music drives on to a boogaloo beat. Ray is mad at the end—"You better listen, I'm trying to tell you something, man."

He lays bare the heart of "Abraham, Martin, and John." "I turned around one day, and they were gone, just like that," Ray mourns after a dramatic electric piano opening. He is close to tears at the end. Ray's version of "Take Me Home, Country Roads" is a one-man hollering match: his overdubbed voice sings the melody, harmonizes with the chorus, shouts to the band, and calls into the living rooms of the country for listeners to join in.

> Country Roads, take me home
> To the place I belong
> West Virginia, mountain mama,
> Take me home, Country Roads.*

Ray shouts, "I like that!" "Me too," responds Ray. Back home on that country road "Every Saturday Night" they drink corn likker from a Mason jar, eat fried fish and homemade food—no

*"Take Me Home, Country Roads" by Bill Danoff, Taffy Nivert & John Denver.
© Copyright 1971—Cherry Lane Music Co. Used by permission. All rights reserved.

wonder he wants to go there. "Butter beans and chitlins too— oooh, every Saturday night. . . . I get so tore down don't even know my name." The message closes with "America the Beautiful." Snare drums and bugles open. "Now when I was in school we used to sing it like this," he says, and then lauds the spacious skies, purple mountains, and fruited plains. "I'm talking about *America*, sweet America, God done shed his grace on thee, he did, he crowned thy good, yes he did, with brotherhood, from sea to shining sea, oh, I wish I had somebody to help me sing this." A chorus joins him. "I love you, America." The record ends with a final, "Thank you, Lord" from Ray, and a roll of kettledrums.

At writing his most recent record is *Through the Eyes of Love*. On the front cover his dark glasses rest on purple cloth. A red rose lies across a photograph of his downcast face on the back. The sounds open with oddly thrashing strings. "There's an aching in my heart." Ray is alone again, "My first night alone without you." The theme is love, lost and gained. "Girl, I'm so lonesome tonight." Sometimes, Ray says, he talks to himself— "Will night go away?" On the Gershwin ballad, "Someone to Watch Over Me," Ray's crooning creates a mood like closing time at a dream nightclub; a single violin follows Ray up to the last high note.

The record closes with a long version (six minutes) of Brook Benton's big hit, "Rainy Night in Georgia," written by Tony Joe White. Ray is alone again, it's "raining all over the world." Neon signs flash, buses pass, a train moans. A guitar player picks, Ray plays the electric piano. "How many times I wondered, it still come out the same." He'll crawl into a boxcar with his guitar, hold her picture close. "I'm just sitting here trying to finish off this half pint." He's getting drunk, and he mumbles as the band draws the song to a close. "If I could get my hands on some Sterno . . . Somebody ought to turn off that water, I mean, ish rainin' all over the world. Aw, shut off that rain!" His voice is gone. "Putting that ending on the record," said Ray Charles, "yes, that was me in one of my sillier moments."

The last bit of applause for Sister Susaye's "Over the Rainbow" had gone to silence. Ray broke it; he grinned broadly as he spoke. "Now we got somebody in here tonight who I hear is saying he ain't paid to see me." Quiet in the hall. "You know who I'm talking about—B. B. King." That brought cheers. "Well I figure if he's gonna *sneak* in to hear me, he's gonna have to come up here and pay the price. B. B.," he called him through the mike, "come on, everybody, help me bring Mr. B. B. King out here."

Half the crowd was on its feet. B. B. strode down the aisle. "Oh, here he comes," said Ray. "Whooopee! Oh, I love B. B., couldn't tell you how I love this man. I'll tell you, if I was a woman, you know, I'd give him a little piece." He laughed. B. B. was on stage. "Okay, plug yourself in now. And we'll get John up here on pie-anna, and I'll move over to this thing"—the electric piano. "Hey, Deacon John, let's go, leave that organ behind." John Henderson left the pit. "Watch the Deacon walk," Ray told everyone. Henderson did step like a churchman. Edgar Willis played a snatch of "Elephant Walk."

Ray hit a note on the electric piano. "That key'll suit you?" he asked B. B. B. hit a few twangy notes in reply. "Well, now, B. B.," said Ray, "I thought we'd play some blues." They were off. Ray started singing "Baby, Please Don't Go," then that got switched into "What'd I Say." Ray eased back the tempo and volume: he had something to say. "See, we wanna give you some of our dirt music, the music from which we come," he said; B. B. agreed on guitar. Deacon John and the Raelets shouted "Amen." The band shook their tambourines and maracas, hit their cowbells. "You can elevate yourself, but you can't get rid of your roots," said Ray. "You always are what you are." A chorus of "Right on!" from crowd and stage alike. B. B. and Ray were back into the blues. Each had his ears cocked to the other. Their phrases flew faster, climaxed, dissolved. Aaron and Freddy were called back. Aaron stood with the Raelets; Freddy's eyebrows waggled to the beat.

"The Ray Charles Show 1972," said Joe Adams' voice through

the public address system. "Ladies and gentlemen, you have been entertained by Mr. B. B. King, the King of the Blues; the fabulous Aaron and Freddy; the world-famed Raelets; and by the Genius himself, Mr. Ray Charles! Let's hear it for them, ladies and gentlemen." Extended cheering.

The crowd got up and started out. The band continued the groove. After their bows Ray and B. B. went back to playing. Half the house had turned their backs, headed home. Ray and B. B. chased each other lickety-split through a dozen howling choruses.

"Oh, B. B., I love you, and you know everybody, it's all right," said Ray. The band took up the refrain. "It's all right, you're all right, we love you, it's all right." Ray stood, hugged himself as he had as the show began. He sat once again and drove the band into "Let's Go Get Stoned." Bob Taylor arrived to lead him off. He went off waving and shouting. "Let's go get stoned, all right! That's what I'm gonna do!"

Me too.